Y0-DNL-744

Words and Actions

An Autobiography

William Buckwalter Smart

Salt Lake City, 2016

© 2016 by William B. Smart
All rights reserved

ISBN:978-1-935821-35-9

Printed and bound by DMT Publishing

Cover photo: William B. Smart as executive editor and
editorial page editor of the Deseret News, 1966.

For Donna

Contents

Preface

In Mitch Albom's book *Have a Little Faith* is a passage that gives me pause. As in his best-selling book *Tuesdays With Morrie,* he is engaged in a series of conversations with a man nearing death—in this case, an aged Jewish rabbi.

What do people fear most about death? he asks the rabbi.

> "Fear?" He thought for a moment. "Well, for one thing, what happens next? Where do we go? Is it what we imagined?"
>
> That's big.
>
> "Yes, but there's something else."
>
> What else?
>
> He leaned forward. "Being forgotten," he whispered.

Fear of being forgotten. Is that reason enough to justify a book like this? No, but there's something else. There's the hope that my posterity will find in its pages evidences and examples of my core beliefs and perhaps may even adopt some of them into their own approach to life. And that historians may be interested in learning how a liberal-leaning editor could hold that position for fifteen years, the longest tenure in the century-old history of the decidedly conservative *Deseret News*.

So this book is offered to both. A core belief that has shaped my life is best stated by W. H. Murray:

> Until one is committed there is hesitancy, the chance to draw back, always ineffectiveness. Concerning all acts of initiative (and creation), there is one elementary truth, the

ignorance of which kills countless ideas and splendid plans: that the moment one definitely commits oneself, then providence moves too. All sorts of things occur to help one that would never otherwise have occurred. A whole stream of events issues from the decision, raising in one's own favor all manner of unforeseen incidents and meetings and material assistance which no man could have dreamt would have come his way.

Along with that, I have learned a deep respect for one of Goethe's couplets:

Whatever you can do, or dream you can, begin it.
Boldness has genius, power and magic in it.

A related core belief is that we are entitled to receive and do receive promptings from a divine source that guide our lives, including whether or not to undertake a project in the first place. The confidence born of these beliefs has led to my acceptance of a challenge I found years ago scrawled on an envelope in a desk in the museum home of Henry Ford:

Dare to do more than you can do
        and do it.
Bite off more than you can chew
        and chew it.
Hitch your wagon to a star, keep your seat,
        and there you are.

Hence the undertakings at the newspaper, in the community, in my church, and in my earth stewardship described in these pages.

Recognition of the profound debt of gratitude and stewardship we owe for this beautiful earth is another of the core beliefs that have shaped my life. In nature, I have come to believe, is soul-renewal. Failure to strive to tune body and spirit to enjoy it—and passing up opportunities to care for it—are sins of ingratitude.

Donna and I or sometimes I alone have been privileged to feel that gratitude in far-distant parts of the earth—the Himalayas, Antarctica, the Drakensberg Mountains of South Africa,

Denali, and many others. More important, we have experienced the soul-cleansing sense of gratitude in our own beloved state of Utah, especially in camping and backpacking in its red-rock wilderness. We have rejoiced in watching our children, grandchildren, and now great-grandchildren grow in love of and sense of stewardship for it.

My own exercise of earth stewardship has led to some of the most rewarding and enjoyable—but in one case frustrating—parts of my life. Fifteen years of service on the Grand Canyon Trust board of directors gave me the privilege of rubbing shoulders with men and women I regard as giants of earth stewardship. The hour spent sitting stop Rainbow Bridge with two of them, marveling at the beauty and majesty all around us and pondering how best to protect it, was life-defining. I feel gratitude for having been the initiator of changes that have made a profound difference in the goals and accomplishments of that organization.

Unarguably, the most life-shaping core belief is faith and activity in the Church of Jesus Christ of Latter-day Saints. Twice my intended career path was changed by calls of service in that church, the first to the governing board of the church youth organization, the second as bishop. Both calls proved a blessing, leaving me to continue my career at the Deseret News. That career gave me the privilege of association with a number of general authorities serving on our board of directors, but most closely with Gordon B. Hinckley and Thomas S. Monson, presidents, in turn, of the company, to whom I reported during my years as editor. I loved and honored these men and am grateful for their leadership and support. I hope my frank discussion in these pages of the problems I faced, not so much with them or other board members but with one or two of their colleagues among the general authorities, will not be seen as disrespect for their callings.

To sum up: Above all of my core beliefs is that God knows and cares for us with unconditional love. He desires all to return to Him, and through the Atonement of his Son and modern revelation has shown and prepared the way.

Acknowledgements

The unsung hero in creation of this book was Richard Christensen, my secretary, confidant, and friend at the Deseret News. He transcribed and typed what became more than a thousand legal-size pages of my dictated daily journal during my editor years. He also assembled, without my knowledge, a bulky scrapbook of my activities. Both were essential to the accuracy of the book.

After that, it was a family affair.

Our grandson Jedediah Rogers, a historian at the Utah Division of State History, read and commented on the content. Our daughter Kristen Rogers-Iversen did copyediting and the book layout. Our granddaughter Hannah Graves did the index and proofed the manuscript with an eagle eye. My wife, Donna, provided wise counsel on the content of the book, gave encouragement throughout, and showed infinite patience while it was in process. To all of them my heartfelt gratitude.

These family members have helped produce this book about my public life. But far beyond that, I owe an enormous debt of gratitude to my entire family. No person stands alone, and a life is not an individual affair. Life is about relationships, and without the people nearest and most beloved to me supporting me, enriching me, and teaching me, my public life could not have unfolded as it did. My parents gave me a foundation of love, security, education, belief in myself, and faith. My siblings and I have had a lifetime of growing together in knowledge, wisdom, and love. Nephews, nieces, cousins, and in-laws all are part of the beautiful web of relationships that is my life.

From their birth to the present, my children have been my teachers and companions, and in a real way, they have helped shape who I am. Each of them has gifts, strengths, and understandings that have challenged me and blessed me. The same is true of their spouses, whom I regard as my children as well. My grandchildren and great-grandchildren have expanded my vision and love infinitely. All the years together and each of the times we have spent together are foundational.

And finally, Donna. With all my experience with words, there are no words to express my love and my debt to this woman. I simply cannot imagine a life without her by my side, and I could not have lived the life I did without her. Unseen behind all my public endeavors, there was Donna. Unsung, she has cared for the practical home and family matters that supported my work. She has always been there to comfort and soothe, to advise and chasten, to provide hope, and to encourage. She has believed in me. She has put up with my failings. She has been a constant beacon and refuge, a full partner, and a brilliant woman of words and action in her own right.

To her, and to all of my family, I humbly acknowledge my debt and reiterate my gratitude and love.

CHAPTER ONE

The Early Years

I n 1922, the year a Fascist march on Rome brought Mussolini to power and the infant Nazi party was beginning its struggle with communists to replace Germany's failing Weimar Republic, I came into the world. Things weren't so great in the USA that year either. The 1921 recession had left five million Americans without jobs. The price of Henry Ford's Model T fell to $290, but we couldn't afford one. Nor could we buy a radio, though the first commercial radio station had opened two years earlier. The first "radio" I can remember was a homemade crystal set.

But back to my birth: The date, June 27. The place, Provo, Utah. My father, Thomas Laurence Smart, and mother, Nelle Buckwalter, had married in 1916 following a discreet courtship while serving as Mormon missionaries in the Northwestern States Mission. I became the fourth of their six children.

First was Margaret, pretty, stylish, perfectionist. Eighteen months later came Mildred, easy-going, outdoorsy, rebellious, adventuresome. Two years after her came Tom, my tormenter in the early years until, around age 12, I rebelled, emerged from the ensuing fistfight with a black eye, but won a lifelong friend. Mary, three years behind me, became in turn the object of my torment, but bore it with a sweet calmness that characterized her until the day of her death in 2004, the first of our siblings to go. Finally came Richard, born after a seven-year gap, precocious but spoiled, largely lost to the family after cocaine cost him his wife and a promising legal/banking career. He moved to France with his French-born second wife, kicked his addiction, and

1

settled, apparently happily, into a modest career as a French-English translator.

To me as a child, our home seemed secure and happy. Not until later years did I realize that Dad's often-disabling asthma and migraine headache attacks probably stemmed from struggling to meet the expectations of a father who had been the righteous giant of Mormon pioneering in the Uinta Basin. A second cause may have been the demands of a wife for luxuries he couldn't provide. Born to a moderately prosperous American Fork farm family, Mother was beautiful and, to me most of the time, angelic. But I remember hoping the neighbors couldn't hear her shrill tirades against my father. Not for years did I learn that Dad's months-long absence one year was because he had left home not knowing if he would return. Nor did I realize at the time that the caning I suffered at his hands on my 12th birthday for lying to my sister came from a man often near the breaking point. (Instead of considering it child abuse, I rather proudly charged neighbor kids a penny to see the welts on my back-side.) I know now why Dad, an accomplished baseball player in his youth, never played catch with us; why I can remember only one camping trip, to Moon Lake in the Uinta Mountains, in all our growing-up years; why only once did Dad take me fishing. He was too spent, emotionally and physically.

But nothing of that did I realize as a child; I knew then only that I loved my parents and they loved me. And as an adult I have felt only love and admiration for the way they stuck it out until, by the time we had reached adulthood and the financial pressures were off, they had become ideal parents and even better grandparents.

The post-World War I years were supposed to be prosperous in America, but in our home they weren't. Dad floundered before my birth and for many years after, as school teacher, farmer, sheepman, furniture finisher, traveling woolen goods salesman, before settling into successful career as a salesman and eventually agency manager for Beneficial Life Insurance Co. We were never hungry during my childhood years, but money was scarce. For example, after kindergarten and first grade in the BYU Training School, I was thrown into the public school system because we could no longer afford the tuition, which may have been around $10 a year.

Another way to stretch dollars as we grew older was to rent

what would have been Tom's and my bedroom to BYU coeds. That meant we slept in a screened-in front porch, which was nice in the summer, listening to the crickets in the big tree just outside. In winter, a hot water bottle made going to bed barely tolerable, but getting up was torture. We would grab our shoes and clothes and dash into the kitchen to get dressed by the coal stove. But there were compensations. The bedroom was in the back of the house on the ground floor, the girls were careless about pulling the blinds, and we learned early to appreciate the beauty of the female body.

We children were expected to help financially, and did. Among my early memories are trudging past the fashionable homes on Provo's University Avenue on bitter cold Sunday mornings, calling out "Salt Lake Tribuuune! Sunday morning paper!" On my return, mother would warm my half-frozen hands in her ample bosom—something no other woman in my life has been willing to do. I bought papers for three cents apiece, sold them for a nickel, and on a good morning might net 25 or 30 cents. Those earnings—minus, sometimes, a five-cent hamburger guiltily purchased at a greasy-spoon joint on University Avenue—went into an account at American Fork Bank, which rewarded my industry and thrift by closing its doors following the 1929 crash. Gone were my life's savings of $7.77. I have always claimed that my newspaper career started at age four or five. My parents in later years insisted I was at least six, and they were probably right.

Other careers followed. I delivered to the neighbors surplus milk from the one or two cows we milked, and peddled the nuts Dad sometimes took in trade for knit goods. We trudged up country lanes to the Pleasant Grove bench to pick strawberries, cherries, and later apples, for a few cents a box. For some years, in my early teens, I peddled magazines—individual copies, not subscriptions—door to door, and can feel even now my embarrassment when a girl I admired at school answered my knock.

At home, it was my job to keep the woodbox behind our cast-iron kitchen range supplied. Suitable kindling was scarce; somehow, I escaped whippings for stealing pickets off our cedar fence. The other detested winter chore was milking. There's a romance to milking sweet-smelling cows fresh from summer pasture. In winter it's different. I remember no romance about washing frozen manure from flanks and udders or squeezing

3

chapped teats and receiving a retaliatory kick by a manure-laden hoof.

In summer there was the drudgery of hoeing weeds in what seemed to be endless rows of our garden. A daily task was the herding of our one or two cows along the unbroken lane that then was Provo's Eighth North from Fourth to Seventh East. We were too poor to afford pasturage, but the ditch banks were lush with grass and edible weeds, and we had no worry about traffic; there was virtually none. I often failed in my responsibilities. While I explored the world's exotic places with Richard Halliburton or mushed under the northern lights with Jack London, or experimented with cedar bark from the fence posts or the weed we called Indian tobacco or dried cow dung to determine which made the least evil-smoking cigarette, the cows often got out of sight. The cows were not fools; we never located them other than in one of the neighbors' corn fields.

Up or down that Eighth North lane, spring or fall, trudged bands of sheep heading to or from grazing on the slopes above Rock Canyon or further east. In spring Dad or, in his frequent absence, Mother would bargain with the herder to buy for a half-dollar or so what we called a "bummer lamb," orphaned from or abandoned by its mother. This we would feed and pet until the inevitable day of slaughter led to suppers of lamb cutlets, which, despite our affection for our former pets, we savored. Not so savored were the tough and stringy mutton stews made from worn-out ewes purchased in the fall.

We lived most of my Provo years on the southeast corner of Eighth North and Third East. Earlier homes I remember were in the Terrace, a long-vanished line of rowhouses on Sixth North between University Avenue and First East, and a rented house on University Ave between Third and Fourth North. Both were close to the Brig-ham Young University Lower Campus, which I furtively explored, gazing with horrified fascination on pickled fetuses in the biology lab.

But the Eighth North home was the first we owned, and to me its location was magical. Across the street to the north began the bench that marked the lowest level of Lake Bonneville, on which now sprawls the BYU campus. Then, the only buildings up on the hill were the library, long since replaced, and the president's home. Up the side of the hill at what is now Seventh East ran a cage housing two cougars, the BYU mascot. Often told to and repeated by us was a story, probably apocryphal, of how older boys threw a dog on top of the cage, where its feet went through the mesh and it was torn to pieces by the cougars.

The best thing about the hill, though, was that it made an ideal batting cage. I spent countless hours tossing up rocks and with a stout stick knocking them from our backyard across the road and up that hill, counting by how far each traveled whether it was a single, double, triple, or home run. Unnumbered are the World Series games I won, usually for the Pittsburgh Pirates, with last-inning, bases-loaded home runs. Whatever hand-eye coordination I have possessed was chiefly developed in those baseball classics.

Sometime around age ten or eleven I found access to a tennis racket, the old wooden variety, far too heavy for a kid that age. I have long answered questions about why I serve left-handed and play right-handed with obscure references to youthful injuries. Now it is time for the truth. Naturally left-handed, I learned to serve and play that way. The racket was so heavy I had to hit ground strokes with both hands. That was many years before Bjorn Borg and others made two-handed strokes respectable, so to escape ridicule I gradually dropped my left hand from the racket and ended up playing right handed. I hung around the BYU tennis courts, worshiping people like Buck and Sanky Dixon and playing when and with whom I could, usually with balls worn down to the rubber. An early highlight, at about age 12 or 13, was beating a ranking player—it may have been Gordon Booth—but only because it was a handicap tournament and I started every game leading 30-love.

Of Provo schools I remember little. The best thing about Parker Elementary School, at Second North and First East but long since demolished, was the outside spiral slide fire escape where, although—or more likely because—it was forbidden, we loved to play. The worst was being beaten up occasionally by Anna Lee Strate, the principal's daughter. I have since reasoned that it must have been because she liked me. (Years later I learned that my future wife, Donna, was a fifth grader at Parker School when her older sister Elaine spent her freshman year at BYU, and that Anna Lee was her best friend.)

Teachers, I learned in that school, can make a huge difference. In fourth grade mine was Miss Nelson, large, middle-aged, red-haired, often red-faced, and demanding. I didn't like her, and the feeling seemed to be mutual. At the end of the school year she reported I was so dim-witted I should be held back to repeat the fourth grade. Mother talked the principal out of that unthinkable fate, and I moved on to the fifth grade. There, the teacher was Miss Davis, petite, dark-haired, young, and beautiful. I adored her. At the end of that year she recommended that I was so bright I should be double-promoted. Wisely, Mother scotched that idea as well.

Farrar Junior High was memorable chiefly because that's where I first played the trumpet and joined the school band; because of a never-forgotten running hook shot that won an inter-class basketball game; and because I pitched and played first base on the baseball team. Dixon, the only other junior high in Provo, was our sole opponent, so beating them was a Big Thing. As for what happened in classrooms, I remember little other than excelling in spelling bees and being bored listening to kids read aloud stuff I had read pages ago. Reading was a passion to me. Before age 12 I persuaded the librarian to give me a card for Provo's upstairs adult library by demonstrating that I had read everything in the basement junior library.

In our home was a 15-volume set of books by John Lord, called *Beacon Lights of History: The World's Heroes and Master Minds*, published three years before my birth. How it got there I do not know; its purchase price would have been far beyond my father's reach. Probably it was gifted by my namesake grandfather, a wealthy man at that time and a lover and collector of books. Whatever the source, I devoured many of the six thousand pages of those books, searching out the heroes more avidly than the master-minds. The *Beacon Lights* still have place in my library, though I spend far less time with them now than in my early teens.

Mine was a sheltered childhood, with little attention paid to events outside our peaceful valley. I remember being shocked by the Lindberg baby kidnapping, but I gave considerably more attention to Babe Ruth's growing home run record. I must have been aware of the Great Depression, but didn't think much about it. We were already pretty poor, and being poorer didn't seem to make much difference. I do remember during the Hoover-Roosevelt election campaign asking my staunchly Republican father what's the difference between Republicans and Democrats? When he explained that Republicans believe more in self-reliance and Democrats believe more in help from the government, I declared with all the political sagacity of a ten-year-old, "Then I guess I'm a Democrat."

At the usual age of eight I was baptized in the old Provo Tabernacle. Bishop Sowards presided over our Manavu Ward for some twenty years. He ran a grocery store, and was either tolerant or ignorant about the candy and small toys we kids stole there—until the day Dad caught me and escorted me to Bishop Sowards to return, with a tearful apology, what was left of my loot. I still remember (and occasionally repeated, many years later during my own service as a bishop) his lecture on the eternal consequences of dishonesty. At age 12 I was ordained a deacon and did what deacons do—pass the sacrament and gather fast offerings—and at age 14 began doing what teachers do—squirm in restless boredom during what were then called block teaching visits with my father. None of it made much impression. Provo was close to 100% Mormon, and I took the Church for granted.

In 1936, though, Dad was given charge of Beneficial Life's Nevada agency, and just before my last year of junior high we moved to Reno. There, I learned about life outside Zion. My ecclesiastical calling, together with fellow-teachers in the tiny Reno Branch, was to prepare the Sacrament. But first we had to empty the ashtrays and sweep out the beer bottles in Dania Hall where we met. After some months of delivering papers for the Reno Evening Gazette, I was given the job of collecting unpaid subscription accounts. My territory included the Stockade, Reno's red light district along the Truckee River. Collecting was hard. The girls were transitory and evasive, and when I did manage to locate a delinquent one, the response was often an invitation to accept payment in kind. That only terrified me; wiser in things no 15-year-old should know about, I soon quit.

I learned in Reno about the power of prayer. One of my Mormon friends, Jimmy Anderson, had a Model T Ford in which he, Eugene Tidball and I spent many hours. Money for gas at sixteen cents a gallon was a constant problem, though, and when we came across a car overturned on a country road, its wheels in the air, we recognized an opportunity. Busy removing the wheels, we didn't see or hear the patrol car, and soon found ourselves being interrogated at the police station. Never before had I prayed so earnestly—first, that I wouldn't go to jail; second, that my parents would never find out. The prayers worked; I didn't, and, until I confessed to them forty years later, they didn't.

There was a discovery, too, about the price of consecration. Loving sports, I pitched, left-handed, on an American Legion baseball team and had got to the finals of the State High School tennis doubles tournament—the latter somewhat less than impressive since the Nevada of 1937 probably contained no more than half a dozen tennis courts. In that year, the LDS Reno Branch, tired of meeting in Dania Hall, set about building the area's first Mormon chapel. It was a do-it-yourself project, and I spent many hours working there. Shingling the roof one day, I stepped on a loose shingle and slid down the roof. The fall was only eight or ten feet, but enough to dislocate my left shoulder. For years after, it slipped out at the most awkward times. That ended my baseball career, and I didn't pick up a tennis racket until years later, at college. Reno had no LDS seminary in those days, but I had heard enough pioneer stories to realize that, tragic as it seemed to me, my trial of faith ranked fairly low on the scale of sacrifice for the gospel's sake.

Strange how I mostly remember adversities and failures. Like the time Gene, Jimmy and I decided we needed a canoe and set about building one. Canvas stretched over a wooden frame was so heavily plastered with tar we could barely lift our creation. The first—and last—voyage was short. Launching in the Truckee River, two paddling while one bailed, we floated grandly under the Reno bridges toward Sparks and, we hoped, on to Pyramid Lake. Somehow we took a wrong turn and found ourselves in a stinking backwater, which turned out to be the Sparks sewer settling pond. Jimmy, whose turn it was to bail, refused, the canoe sank, we floundered ashore, and made our way back to the river to scrub ourselves and our clothes. For all I know, the canoe is still there.

Then there was my musical career. Back in the days before the Mormon Church banned brass instruments in Sacrament Meeting, I played trumpet solos there—"The Holy City" was a favorite—and considered myself pretty good. Now it was time to prove it. For months I labored over a difficult composition for the state high school music competition in what in 1938 was the tiny desert town of Las Vegas. Waiting my turn in the pre-air conditioning heat, I was confident I had the piece down cold. Then someone reported there was a telegram for me in the

Western Union office. Fearing the worst, I raced there, read the telegram, which said Good luck, etc., and raced back, breathless and soaked in sweat, just in time to hear my name called. The first movement was a disaster, but I recovered in time to get a rating of "excellent," which, considering that everyone else I ever heard of was rated "superior," was roughly equivalent to a D minus.

A month later, in Los Angeles for the western region music festival, I was going to redeem myself. The marching band competition was in the 100,000-seat Los Angeles Coliseum, built only a few years before for the 1932 Olympics. To this day I'm certain—well, almost certain—we were supposed to repeat the first movement of our Sousa march. So I did, but the band didn't. For a dozen measures my solo trumpet rang out in that vast stadium as I expected the others to realize their mistake and join in. They didn't, and at last, in confusion and shame, I quit. That pretty well sums up my musical career. My trumpet lived on through the careers, in turn, of two grandsons, Spencer and Will Rogers, both of whom became much better than I.

I've always maintained that my personality and self-confidence were stunted in those formative years because each time I started to amount to something I had to start over in a new location. That happened when, after climbing the social ladder during two years of junior high school in Provo, I suffered the last year as a nobody at Billinghurst Junior High in Reno. It happened again when, after I had achieved modest status at Reno High School, Dad was made Beneficial Life's general agent for the Pacific Northwest. So, in the summer of 1938, we moved to Portland, and what was supposed to be a glorious senior year of high school was spent in obscurity.

But there were compensations. For the first time, the Church became important to me—socially if not spiritually. I was now 16, at the age to discover girls, and here in Portland were wonderfully exciting Mormon girls to discover. My previous experience, except for childhood games of Spin the Bottle, had been confined to a single and certainly chaste goodnight kiss with Viola Wittwer on the porch of the home in Sparks where she was visiting. Still today, I have a vivid memory of the dizziness left by that first kiss as I wove my way to the bus stop. (Years later, at age 82 I was High Priest Group leader in the Ensign Second Ward in Salt Lake City and recruited Marion

Wittwer as our secretary. Naturally, I asked if he knew Viola Wittwer, learned she was his sister, and was immensely gratified when he later reported that she, too, remembered that kiss.)

Other kisses with the Portland girls followed, of course, though none, as I recall, much less chaste than that first one. Lack of cars was one reason. I had no car of my own; none of us did. Moreover, I had precious little use of the family car, probably because years earlier my older sister Margaret as a teenager had wrecked the first new car our father had bought. So most of our courting was on foot or by bus, not the best setting for serious romance. Another obstacle was that the girl who interested me most, Blanche Petersen, lived way out on 82nd Street off Sandy Boulevard, too far to walk, and the buses didn't run after midnight.

I bore another heavy handicap in the dating game. Portland, like most of Oregon, is blessed with beautiful deepwater lakes. Kids reared there learn to swim from early childhood. But until my mid-teens I grew up in Provo, where Utah Lake, our only one, was shallow, turgid, smelly with sewage from the nearby towns. We never swam there; in fact, in those years I never swam anywhere. So, shivering on the Lake Oswego boat dock, watching those beautiful Portland girls dive and flash through the water like lissome mermaids, was a torment. Eventually, someone pushed me in. I floundered to shore and became, from that moment, a swimmer, though never a good one.

On terra firma, two events stick in memory. One was a fathers-and-sons softball game at an overnight outing on Mount St. Helens, years before it blew up. My father, playing second base, made a nice grab of a hard-hit grounder and threw the runner out at first. As I first drafted this chapter, in my late eighties and still playing moderately competitive tennis, I smiled at the memory of my pride and astonishment that an old man like that—he was 45—could make such a play. Another fond memory of those late-teen years is of the annual Thanksgiving Morning "Mud-Bowl" touch-football games against the ward's young-marrieds. I was our principal go-to pass receiver, and felt pardonable pride the one year we beat those older guys.

What should have been a climactic senior year, at Portland's Washington High School, was remarkably forgettable. It was a big, impersonal school. As a new student there I was an unknown, and, except for competing, unsuccessfully, for first chair in the trumpet section of the school orchestra, did little or nothing to become known. But, mercifully, the year passed, and in June 1939, after equally forgettable commencement exercises, I emerged from the cocoon of public schooling only modestly prepared to face the future.

Bill (l), Tom, Mary, and cousin play in the snow; Bill and Tom and Mary with their mother; Bill and Tom with a calf.

Bill as fireman for a day, in high school in Reno; high school graduation picture.

CHAPTER TWO

Lurching into Adulthood

Finally out of high school, I faced a choice. I could go on to a public college—perhaps Oregon State University where my older brother went. But for now-unremembered reasons I had resolved to attend Reed College, a small, private, liberal arts school in Portland. Its tuition was prohibitively expensive, the scholarship offered was small, and by then the established family principle was that we were to make our own way; there would be no parental money for private college tuition So the only way I could go to Reed was to stay out of school for a year, get a job, and earn the money needed. But I was determined, so that's what I did.

The job I found was with Lincoln Electric Company, then and still today the world's largest manufacturer of arc welding machines and welding rods. Ours was a small sales and distributing operation on a railroad siding in a seedy industrial area of northwest Portland, a long bus ride from home. But for me, the job became a life-changer.

Up to that time, I had done little to build self-confidence or a sense of responsibility. What money I had earned had come from mowing lawns, delivering or collecting for newspapers, peddling magazines, picking fruit—small-change stuff any kid could do. Now, at age 18, I was thrust into a position of serious responsibility with the authority that goes with it.

Ours was a three-man staff: the manager, who spent much of his time calling on customers; a salesman, who spent all of his time doing so; and me. My job was warehouse manager and shipping clerk, plus answering phones and serving walk-in customers when I was the only one in the front office. I managed the inventory, ordering the kinds and sizes of welding rods as needed. I chose which trucking companies to call for out-of-town shipments, and, of course, prepared those shipments. For local deliveries I engaged a wise old man with his pickup truck. He became a friend and confidant who taught me much. After he died, his son delivered as his bequest to me his shaving brush and straight-edge razor. I kept them for many years.

Periodically, a freight car would appear on our siding, loaded with around 800 fifty-pound cans of welding rods and a dozen or so welding machines. That's when I became not just an employee, but a boss. I usually hired two burly Mormon friends, Don Magleby and Gene Mattice, both of whom were in college but could work on Saturday. Supervising as well as joining in their work, seeing that the rods were appropriately stacked by type and size, was just one of the elements in that employment that built in me a sense of self-worth and confidence. The job was challenging and often stressful. It was just what I needed.

As fall 1940 approached, I gave notice; I was leaving to go to college. The boss tried to dissuade me, explaining that Lincoln Electric had a policy of keeping salaries modest—mine was $80 a month—but after a year on the job giving a Christmas bonus equal to a year's salary. By leaving I would walk away from $960. To me, that was a fortune. But by then I knew this was no career for me, and enrolled at Reed College as an over-age freshman.

CHAPTER THREE

Life-Shaping at Reed

Looking back, I am struck by how key decisions of my early adulthood led step by step to my career, without my having any clue that I was going there. Choosing Reed was one of these. Reed was no ordinary college. Founded in 1911 on lovely farm and woodlands in what would become Portland's upscale Eastmoreland section, it set a new and different course from the beginning. Its founding president, William T. Foster, was at 31 the nation's youngest college president. He assembled its youngest faculty, idealists from elite eastern colleges attracted to Reed by Foster's vision of intellectual purity and vigor, academic freedom, meritocracy, nonconformity, and acquisition of knowledge for knowledge's sake. That formula seemed to work. Reed's first five graduating classes produced three Rhodes scholars, and for decades it continued to produce them at the nation's highest rate.

By the time I arrived in 1940, Foster was long gone, but his basic principles were well established. A senior thesis and a rigorous oral exam were mandatory for graduation. No grades were given out except by request after graduation; we didn't study for grades, but to learn. In four years there I never had an indication of where I stood, and the announcement at commencement exercises that I had been elected to Phi Beta Kappa came as a total surprise.

An honor system, never codified lest it become sclerotic, governed our social as well as academic behavior. On two occasions, because of schedule conflicts I was allowed to take a critical examination on my own, with no one around to check on whether I peeked at my notes or textbooks. I never did, and was never aware of anyone else violating the trust placed in us. (By sad contrast, in a 2010 survey of 14,000 college undergraduates, two-thirds acknowledged cheating on tests or homework.)

Foster banned the distractions of fraternities or inter-collegiate sports competition. By my time, the fraternity ban re-mained, but the intercollegiate sports ban had been modified, though only marginally. The school's entire athletic staff consisted of one elderly and much-loved man named Botsford. There were no coaches. A student appointed for each sport and called a "master" did what coaching was done, if any, as well as acting as team captain and manager, responsible for arranging games and getting enough people there to play them. Probably because no one else was willing to take it on, I filled that role for basketball during my freshman and sophomore years. We played other small colleges—Linfield, Pacific, and even Whitman from faraway Walla Walla—and on rare occasions managed to win a game. Inept as the basketball team was, the football team was worse. In the post-war years, Reed boasted the nation's longest record of consecutive losses, stretching, as I remember, over three years. Working on the *Oregonian* sports desk during my last year of college, I wrote a story that reached the national wires about how outraged the student body felt over a flukey win that spoiled such a distinguished record.

Though intercollegiate athletic competition languished, intramural competition was intense. Botsford—"Bots" to all of us—worked diligently to get students involved by organizing competitions. One of my fondest college memories is of our six-man touch-football team composed of three faculty members—Bob Rosenbaum, math; Dick Jones, history; Frank Kiernan, humanities—and three students. It was a different kind of game, with unlimited forward passing, often played with a slippery ball in the rain we called "Oregon mist." Probably because of the maturity and cunning of those faculty members as well as a special teacher-student bond, we were never beaten.

My most horrifying moment of those days also involved Rosenbaum. On the squash court, I spun to dig a shot out of the corner and launched a ball that struck him just below the eye. Those who know the heft and hardness of a squash ball know how devastating a hit half an inch higher would have been.

Rosenbaum taught a class that helped shape my future career. I have always struggled with mathematics, but for some reason, possibly because we were football teammates, took his class in non-Euclidean geometry. Without trying to reconstruct it, the basic outline was this: Euclid in 300 B.C. wrote a book, *The Elements*, with Five Postulates that for almost every century since have been the accepted foundation of geometry, based on the concept that space is flat. But in the nineteenth century two alternate systems emerged. Nikolai Lobachevsky hypothesized that space is hyperbolic, Bernhard Riemann that it is elliptical. Both developed valid systems of geometry based on those postulates. Later, Einstein's General Theory of Relativity substantiated those theories and changed forever our concept of the universe.

For me, the message of that class is not mathematical, which is way beyond my comprehension, but philosophical. It is that things may not be what they appear; that known facts may not be that at all; that alternate causes and meanings must be examined; that minds must remain open. These are essential characteristics to which every journalist should aspire.

Indeed, what a more progressive nation and safer world ours would be if instead of being locked into partisan or nationalistic or religious dogmas, leaders and their followers recognized that most of what is "fact" is merely perspective, and that one's perspective is (or ought to be) constantly evolving.

Another life-shaping influence for me was Reed's core curriculum, built around the humanities. In the mid-1920s, one of America's first Rhodes scholars, Richard F. Scholz, became Reed's second president. He introduced a Socratic-type study of the whole human experience to achieve a unified understanding of contemporary life. The purpose he outlined was to equip students to play an active civic role in addressing social problems; to provide them with a broad and socially-minded context for narrower professional training; and to help them attain the art of living fully with their hearts and minds.

Abdominal surgery took his life after two short years as president, and for a decade the faculty, administration, and regents battled over the direction the college should take. By 1940, when I arrived, the faculty had essentially won. The Scholz vision survived. Liberal arts students were required to take a two-year prescribed humanities course starting with the classics and examining man's experience and development over the centuries, including his achievements in literature and the arts. (Only one year was required for science majors.)

It's impossible to define—or, perhaps, to overstate—how profoundly that course and that approach to learning influenced my life and career. One indication may have come when, sixty-nine years later, I unwrapped a birthday gift, *The Art of Living: The Classic Manual on Virtue, Happiness and Effectiveness by Epictetus*. I glanced at the cover and impressed my grand-children—and surprised myself—by identifying the author as a Roman Stoic philosopher. Epictetus was only a minor philo-sopher among those we encountered in that humanities course. But, re-reading his short, pungent messages, I am struck by how they encapsulate principles on which I have tried to build my professional career and, indeed, my life. Even more profound is the evidence that long-forgotten learning and experience are stored somewhere deep in these marvelous brains of ours and subconsciously shape who and what we become.

A third Reed College influence on my future life was the class in western history taught by Dorothy Johansen. Under her tutelage, I wrote an essay, "Oregon and the Mormon Problem," that won second prize in the prestigious Armitage Competition in Pioneer History of the Oregon Country. That achievement, the pride of seeing it published in the Reed College Bulletin, and the cash award that followed cemented my resolve to be a college history professor. Interesting how some events foreshadow the future. My then-recent bride, Donna, while visiting family in Salt Lake City, did important original research for that essay in the LDS Church History Archives. Half a century later she and I collaborated in that same way to produce a book, *Over the Rim: The Parley P. Pratt Exploring Expedition to Southern Utah, 1849-50*, which won the Mormon History Association's 2000 Docu-mentary of the Year Award.

Reed's was—and is—primarily a residential campus, where students found sociality and intellectual stimulus in housing units or various clubs. But some of us, the less affluent, known as "day-dodgers," lived at home and commuted to the campus by bus or on foot. Deprived of a residential campus environment, a few of us compensated by forming what we called the Reed College Pinochle and Whist Club. The name is deceptive. None of us knew anything about Whist, only that it sounded so tweedish. Nor was it really a club; there was no organization, and membership was floating. But we did know Pinochle, and we played it with passion, though never for money; none of us had enough of that to risk.

What was really important about what we called the P & W was that it rooted us socially in the college environment, providing, for me at least, the only lasting college friendships. It served a higher purpose as well. Often, especially as Humanities exams loomed, instead of or after pinochle our sessions became late-night group reviews of lecture notes and assigned readings, with searching discussion of the meaning of it all. I'm confident those sessions helped all of us to meet the intellectual challenge we faced. For me, as the self-assigned leader of those discussions, they brought deeper understanding, self-confidence, and commitment to an academic life.

The Japanese attack on Pearl Harbor plunged America overnight into war and soon changed untold millions of lives. For me, the change was both immediate and life-long. I was tired of washing dishes in the college cafeteria. But to this day I cannot understand why, other than a prompting from a higher source, I would approach the manager of the two-man International News Service Portland bureau and ask with the war breaking out whether he needed more help? INS lagged far behind Associated Press and United Press, and perhaps it couldn't afford anyone better than an inexperienced college sophomore. Or the fact that the manager, George L. Scott, was also the LDS Church Portland Stake president and a close friend of my father may have had something to do with it. Whatever the reason, I got the job.

It wasn't much of one. While still carrying a full class load, I worked from midnight to 8 a.m., monitoring the teletype machines, occasionally writing a local angle into a national story for the benefit of our client newspapers and radio stations, listening to the police radio and writing and filing the rare story that could be gathered by telephone during those hours. Mostly it was tedium, with time for study and catnaps, with one ear alert to the teletype bell signaling that something was coming that needed attention.

The summer of 1942 brought a dramatic change. I was sent to Seattle to cover vacation shifts for the two-man INS bureau. Shortly after my arrival, a heart attack claimed the bureau manager, and his assistant, a Navy reservist, was called to active duty. Replacements were unavailable; for most of the summer I alone was the Seattle INS bureau.

Those were exciting times in the Northwest. On June 3, 1942, planes from two Japanese carriers bombed Dutch Harbor on Unalaska Island, only 800 miles from Anchorage. Three days later, Japanese troops occupied Sitka and Attu Islands, far out at the end of the Aleutian chain. We had no troops there, and the sparse population of Aleuts offered no resistance. With bases on the Aleutians, Japanese submarines could control shipping on the Arctic Great Circle route and prevent a U.S. attack on Japan over that route. Also, it was feared, from there the enemy could launch aerial attacks against the Pacific Northwest, to say nothing of high-altitude balloons to drop fire bombs on the Northwest forests. In the dark early days of the war, even an attack on the mainland was not unthinkable.

The Navy dispatched a cruiser/destroyer force to destroy Japanese supply convoys, after which the enemy could supply its troops only by submarine, and the threat was reduced. In May 1943 our forces retook Attu in a bloody battle that cost 580 American lives (in addition to 318 from non-combat causes) but cost the enemy far more. Of some 2,300 Japanese troops then on the island, their final banzai attack left only 28 alive to be taken prisoner. Shortly after, our invading force to retake Sitka found it abandoned. By then I was in uniform myself.

As a one-man staff reporting on action more than a thousand miles away, I had to rely on what information could be coaxed from army and navy public relations officers. As in much of the reporting of World War II, the public learned only what the military wanted it to learn—one of several reasons World War II is remembered with patriotic nostalgia instead of with the horror brought into our living rooms from more recent ones.

One story I covered that summer was different, though. It came from a news conference in Seattle, where Henry Kaiser and Howard Hughes announced a partnership to build a giant seaplane to convey troops and supplies to Europe, avoiding the carnage from German submarines preying on our freighters in the North Sea. It was to be a huge craft, with cargo capacity of two railroad boxcars, powered by eight 4,000-horsepower engines, each driving a four-blade, seventeen-foot propeller. Its 320-foot wingspan would be the greatest ever, its 70-foot height the tallest. To be built of wood because of wartime metal shortage, it was nicknamed the Spruce Goose, though the wood used was mostly birch.

The contract called for three of these monsters to be delivered within two years. Controversy and delays caused Kaiser's withdrawal to concentrate on building Liberty ships, which he did at an average rate of one every 45 days. Hughes pushed on with the Spruce Goose and finally, after five years rather than two, produced the first–and only–prototype. On 2 November 1947, two years after the war ended, with Hughes himself at the controls, it took its trial flight, lasting all of one mile. It never flew again, and today rests in the Evergreen Aviation Museum near McMinnville, Oregon. Though it ended in utter failure, the Spruce Goose provided for the nation an exciting and hopeful story in the war's darkest days. For me, additional excitement was in seeing in print my first byline.

When I returned to school in the fall of 1942, our sophomore year became an anxious one. Most of us had enlisted in the Army or Navy reserve (Army for me) and expected an active-duty call at any time. In the spring of 1943 the calls came. The P & W gang gathered at the home of Bill Krause, where his tolerant and empathetic mother cooked a farewell dinner featuring wild mallards we had harvested with golf clubs on a moonless night around the lake of the Eastmoreland Golf Course.

With varying degrees of emotion, we parted that night, not knowing who of us would return. Remarkably, we all did. Warren Roberts, Fred Steed and Tom Conway went on to become college professors, Krause a Presbyterian minister, Bob Noel a lumber merchant, Don Magleby an early heart attack victim in New York. Then there was Frank Curtis. Without any religious credentials to validate his convictions as a conscientious objector, he was convicted of draft evasion and sentenced to the McNeil Island federal prison in the southern arm of Puget Sound. Those of us familiar with his stubborn non-conformity were not surprised to learn he escaped, apparently became one of the few ever to survive a long swim through those cold, choppy waters, and became a Reed College folk hero. The last I heard, he was living his own kind of independent life in the high desert country of southeast Oregon.

CHAPTER FOUR

How I Fought the War

My World War II military career fell quite a few medals short of heroic. Mainly, it was a series of training camps in places where I would prefer not to live—Missouri, Arkansas, Texas, Oklahoma, Georgia. But there were highlights in places as diverse as the high plains of Wyoming, where I received the greatest blessing of my life, and Hawaii, where the blessing blossomed. Several fortuitous events spared me anything close to combat.

My April 1943 induction at Camp Adair, Oregon, was followed by an interminable troop train ride to Atlantic City. By the time of our arrival, the luxury resort Traymore Hotel on the boardwalk, known as the Taj Mahal of Atlantic City, had become a vast military barracks. In our six weeks of Signal Corps basic training there, we learned that KP duty in such a place is no less dreary than peeling potatoes anywhere else, and calisthenics in the sand of a beach resort no less exhausting. (In 1972, the Traymore Hotel, deteriorating along with Atlantic City itself, disappeared in the largest controlled implosion up to that time.)

My next assignment was with a Signal Corps unit at Camp Crowder, near Neosho in southwest Missouri. It was a brief one, but long enough for a promotion to corporal. Two stripes may seem fairly insignificant, but in the army's hierarchical culture they gave me meaningful status among my less-favored associates. As it turned out, those stripes may have saved my life.

In December 1942 the army began what was called the Army Specialized Training Program (ASTP). Its purpose, supposedly, was to supply the flow of high-grade technicians and specialists as well as junior officers the army needed. Within a year, 200,000 soldiers were being trained in engineering, science, and foreign languages in 227 colleges around the country at an ultimate cost of $127 million. The program had its critics. One general claimed that the real purpose of ASTP was to save colleges from going bankrupt due to the wartime drain of college-age men. Another complained that despite the critical shortage of potential officers trained for combat, the army was sending such men to college. In June 1943 I became one of these. Judging from my experience in the program, I conclude that the critics were correct.

My entrance into the program was inauspicious. From the heat of a Missouri summer, clad in summer khakis, we detrained at midnight in Laramie into the face of a Wyoming June blizzard. The hike through that blizzard to our quarters in a former women's dormitory on the University of Wyoming campus came as close to making me a casualty as anything in my army experience.

Our assignment was primarily to study Spanish, along with classes in geography and political science. The purpose, we were told, was to prepare us for service in military intelligence or military government. That explanation seemed only vaguely credible, considering that our enemies spoke German, Italian, Japanese, or, possibly some time in the future, Russian.

Not that we complained. Our weekly work load of 24 hours in the classroom and 24 hours of study seemed like a vacation after carrying a full classload at Reed while working at a job almost full-time. Instead of calisthenics, the six hours of required physical exercise often meant rousing touch football and basketball games against our engineering counterparts. As for the required five hours of military instruction, I don't recall experiencing any of it.

In Laramie I came to realize the depth of racial intolerance outside of the South. As chairman, I arranged for a band from Fort Warren near Cheyenne to play at a dance to be sponsored by our language group. They were all African Americans and all, of course, in uniform. I canvassed every hotel, rooming house, and even flop houses near the railroad, for overnight housing. No one would accept them. Finally, we installed bunks in the gymnasium. What most shamed me was the stoicism with which they accepted the situation; it was what they had come to expect.

Useless as it was to the war effort, ASTP was for its members a gift. It kept us out of, or at least postponed, combat. Deprived of the usual male students, the Wyoming coeds were, to say the least, friendly. By contrast with almost every other military base I experienced, the Wyoming summer was cool and mercifully free of the curse of chiggers. The winter, though harsh, was beautiful. Compared to what was going on overseas, life seemed good.

For me, the gift was far greater. Nearing the end of the program and after the breakup of a romantic relationship with a prominent sorority leader, I had a prompting, rare in those days, to attend LDS Sunday services. Providentially, it was the monthly Fast Sunday, with its testimony meeting. Something about a voice behind me bearing testimony in the Mormon way caused me to spin around to look.

In that moment came a distinct impression: This was the girl I was going to marry. She was Donna Toland, a scholarship student from Afton, Wyoming. She was beautiful, intelligent, gifted, firmly grounded in her faith and moral standards. More-over, her father owned a ranch in beautiful Star Valley, Wyoming. And when we went out to dinner she gave me her ice cream. Who could ask for more than all that? Our few dates in the brief weeks before I was to ship out were enough to convince me that my first intuition was inspired.

As conceived, ASTP was to be eighteen months of intensive, accelerated study ending in a college degree and commission as an officer. Its director testified to a Congressional investigating committee that its schedule was more demanding than either West Point or the Naval Academy. Judging by our experience, that was clearly false, and evidence was mounting that it contributed little or nothing to the war effort. So, the plug was pulled. In March 1944 all of us Spanish-trained potential military intelligence officers were shipped to Fort Leonard Wood, Missouri, to become real soldiers in the 97th Infantry Division. Among the 110,000 ASTP students shipped into combat units that spring were people like Robert Dole, Henry Kissinger, Edward Koch, Gore Vidal, Andy Rooney, Roger Mudd, and Mel Brooks.

Whipping a bunch of college boys into battle-ready infan-trymen required merciless discipline, and that's what we got. Our strenuous training in every phase of infantry warfare in-cluded three weeks of practicing amphibious landings on Pismo Beach near San Luis Obispo, California.

My corporal stripes among all those privates gave me additional leadership training and responsibility, which is prob-ably why, shortly before the 97th was shipped to the European

Theater, I was reassigned to become cadre to train new infantrymen, another unsought reason I was spared the perils of combat. Months of that duty at Camp Chaffee, Arkansas, and Camp Gordon, Georgia, grew repetitious and boring, and I applied, successfully, to become an Officer Candidate at the Infantry School, Ft. Benning, Georgia.

In early April 1945 the 97th crossed the Rhine and took a position on the south bank of the Sieg River. On April 7, units of the division crossed that river, bypassing and leaving untouched a building marked with a red cross. However, it wasn't a hospital, but a strongly fortified arms factory. German troops emerged from their tunnels to pour deadly fire into the Americans' rear while others fired from the front. The 97th units involved took eighty percent casualties, dead and wounded. I have never learned how many of my ASTP classmates died that day while I was struggling but safe at Officers Candidate School.

OCS was a three-month torture to produce what the troops derisively called "90-day wonders." It tested us physically to and, for many, beyond the limit. I have always been grateful that then and for many years later I was unaware that I suffered from a birth defect that left a hole in the septum between my right and left atria. The condition is called an atrial septum defect. About half the blood pumped by my heart recirculated through the lungs instead of flowing throughout the body where it belonged. Had I known this, I could never have survived the physical demands of OCS or the equally rigorous Infantry basic training, but would have allowed myself to become an invalid. Not knowing, I pushed harder and excelled, and have never forgotten the truth that what we can achieve is determined far more by what's in the mind and spirit than by what's in the body.

Near the end of OCS, every candidate was required to write an essay on leadership. Taking a cue from the Infantry School motto of "Follow Me" as seen on signs throughout Ft Benning, I wrote of the humble carpenter who arose from his workbench beside the Mediterranean two thousand years ago to launch a world-changing career of leadership based on those same words. It was chosen from among the finalists, and at graduation exercises I delivered that talk to the three companies of newly-minted officers.

Two momentous events occurred during those OCS months. On April 12, at his beloved Warm Springs resort in Georgia,

Franklin D. Roosevelt succumbed to a cerebral hemorrhage. Many of us felt that FDR was our greatest national hero, for his leadership through the Depression and history's bloodiest war. Just four weeks later, we rejoiced that the European part of that war ended with the May 8 surrender of Germany and collapse of the Third Reich.

But for me, an even more important life-shaping event was developing. In the months after the ASTP left Laramie, Donna and I had exchanged a stream of letters that led to a very tentative engagement to be married, but not until sometime after the war. I wanted something more binding than that and wrote to her LDS Institute director, Roy A. Welker, whom she loved and admired, asking him to present an engagement ring. At the final banquet of Lamba Delta Sigma, which she served as president, he made the presentation, accompanied by a beautifully meaningful message. She could hardly decline, and didn't.

Years later, when in his mid-nineties he died, his daughter called to say that he had requested that both of us speak at his funeral to be held in the Paris Idaho Stake Tabernacle, where he had served as stake president. Full of gratitude for his contribution to our life together, we gladly did so.

It would take more than just that good man, though, to bring Donna to the altar. When she graduated from college, I, a brand-new infantry officer, persuaded her to accompany me to Portland to become acquainted with my family. In a few days there she fell in love with them and they with her. On the morning before I was to leave for my next post, in Texas, Dad came to my bedroom.

"We think you should marry that girl now," he began. "You can never know what the war will bring, and she's far too good to risk losing." I agreed but pointed out that her parents were opposed to marriage before war's end, and Donna respected their wishes.

"Well, let's go talk with her."

Dad was an insurance salesman, a good one, and by the time all her objections had been dissected, she was yielding. My sister Mildred's offer to loan us her car until her husband returned from overseas sealed the deal.

Somehow, four of us, including my plump Mother, crowded into the single seat Chevy coupe with balding tires for the 750-mile drive to Star Valley. My barracks bag served as a seat in the rear luggage space. After stopping in Pocatello for an Idaho marriage license, since Wyoming required a three-day waiting period, we reached Afton, where Donna's parents met their future son-in-law for the first time. When we produced our license there were no more objections, and her brothers and sisters and their spouses were called down from a fishing camp on Greys River.

The Idaho-Wyoming state line runs down the main street of the little town of Freedom. There, on July 15, 1945, on Bishop Robinson's front lawn on the Idaho side, he married us. A hastily arranged wedding dinner at the Valleon Hotel followed, and we were off for a two-night-and-one-day straight-through drive to Camp Maxey on the Texas-Oklahoma border. On the second morning, driving east with the rising sun in my eyes, I fell asleep and veered off the road. Providentially, the Texas landscape was flat, there was no barrow pit, fence or telephone pole, and, wide awake by now, I simply drove back onto the road and continued on.

There's a Utah saying that "You should marry a girl from Sanpete (or Dixie or wherever) because no matter how bad it gets, she's had it worse." That's exactly opposite from Donna's first weeks of marriage. How can it be worse for a girl from high and cool Star Valley than arriving exhausted in Texas mid-summer heat, renting a cockroach-infested, share-the-bath room, not knowing a soul in town, and then having her new husband leave the next day for a two-week bivouac?

Well, yes, for a Mormon girl with a new Mormon husband it could get worse. He could return with SenSen failing to disguise the fact that he had washed away the bivouac dust with a single cold beer. What kept Donna from catching the next train home I never knew. That she didn't, I am eternally grateful. One thing became instantly and abundantly clear, though; I would never have another beer or anything like it.

Our first few months were rocky. Dad had counseled Donna in the patriarchal Mormon way that I was to be head of the family, that she should heed my counsel, etc. That didn't sit well with her. There were some stormy sessions before we reached an agreement: I could be head of the family if she could be co-head. That has worked out remarkably well in the nearly seventy years since.

My first three months as an infantry officer were spent whipping my platoon into shape as a combat unit. After that, we understood, we would be on our way to Okinawa. But on August 6, 1945, a B-29 crew trained at Wendover Air Force Base dropped the atomic bomb over Hiroshima that killed 90,000 Japanese that day, with another 75,000 dead within three months. Three days later another atomic bomb over Nagasaki killed 60,000 to 80,000 more, and on August 15 Japan surrendered. Horrible and portentous as we knew this introduction of nuclear warfare to be, we rejoiced that it spared America the bloodbath that an invasion of Japan would surely have been.

In late September orders arrived: Report to Fort Lawton (near Seattle) for shipment overseas. No destination listed; occupation duty in Okinawa or Japan seemed most likely. En route, we stopped in Salt Lake City for an ordinance considered essential by Mormons—the temple sealing of our marriage for eternity. Arriving without a temple recommend, I was subjected to a searching interview by Apostle Charles A. Callis, who, understanding and sympathetic with the exigencies of wartime, signed off on my worthiness and himself performed the ordinance.

At Ft. Lawton, on October 10, I boarded the *General Butner*, one of our largest troop transports, arriving at Pearl Harbor a week later. From there, most of the some 5,000 troops went on to Okinawa, but some, mostly officers including me, left the ship to serve out their enlistments in Hawaii. I was posted to Fort Kamehameha, established in 1907 to house coastal batteries guarding Pearl Harbor. When I arrived, it was serving as a Separation Center, and that became my job—processing the discharge of veterans from the service.

The next three months were, for me, a mixture of boredom in a desk job contrasted with delight in the beauty of Hawaii, the luxury of the Fort DeRussy officers club on Waikiki, beach cookouts and other social events with Mormon servicemen, nurses, and civil service secretaries; basketball, tennis, and determined (but unsuccessful) attempts at surfboarding. For Donna, teaching high school in the icy grip of a Star Valley winter, life was considerably less exciting. For both of us, deeply in love as evidenced in a steady stream of letters, there was growing frustration in being apart.

The army made an offer: Sign on for eighteen more months and we'll bring your wife over at our expense and provide housing. But bring her over on your own without signing up and there will be no housing and you can expect to be transferred farther west. For months we sought a way to beat that game but could find none. Finally, I could wait no longer. In a burst of optimism, or faith, that things would work out, I wrote to Donna: Hang the expense. Get on the first available ship or airplane and come. We'll worry about housing when you get here.

She did, arriving February 20 on the *SS Aleutian*, sunburned to the point of untouchability. That didn't keep us from going boating with friends the next day off Waikiki. Unaware that she couldn't swim, Bob Crandall playfully pushed her overboard. I reached her before she went down for the second time. Back aboard, she reminded me that having saved her life I was forever responsible for her. That was fine with me, since I had never thought otherwise.

For awhile I didn't do too good a job of it, though. The first couple of weeks Capt. Max Rogers (who later became a professor of philosophy at University of Utah) and his wife crowded us into their apartment at Schofield Barracks. When that became intolerable, I brought her to my corner of the Bachelor Officers Quarters, hanging a blanket for privacy. Things were getting desperate; the presence of a monkey that also lodged there didn't help.

But then, strangely, things did work out. I had been the doubles partner of a Hickam Field Air Force major in a Pacific Area tennis tournament (we lost in the third round, I in the second round of singles). He knew of the imminent departure of the officer in charge of VIP (Very Important People) housing at Hickam. Somehow, he pulled the proper strings, and I became probably the only living infantry officer responsible for Air Force VIP housing. Quickly and thankfully, we set up housekeeping in the middle unit of a six-apartment complex.

Our guests often were general-grade officers, members of Congress, or other officials en route to or returning from our atomic testing on Kwajalein Atoll in the Marshall Islands. On our first night, we learned about the nature of our expected duties when, at midnight, the door burst open downstairs and a tipsy general officer roared: "Lieutenant! Where's the booze? Where're the women?"

It's a bit disconcerting for a lowly lieutenant in his pajamas to explain to a three-star general that there would be no more procuring here, either of booze or women. I expected an immediate transfer. It didn't come, possibly because a sobered-up general realized that demanding it could cause a scandal.

Our days—and nights—became idyllic. With orderlies to do the actual work and plenty of time on my hands, I sharpened my tennis and golf games. While I labored at that, Donna got a job as secretary to the commander of the Air Force Transport Command. In my permanently assigned jeep, on her days off we explored every corner of Oahu. On frequent trips to the LDS Temple in Laie, we began to understand the beauty and eternal meaning we had missed in the exhaustion of our first temple experience in Salt Lake City. Beach parties and other socials with the many Mormon couples by then on the island enlivened our lives. After three months of that arduous duty, the military deemed we deserved rest and recreation and sent us to the Big Island to an R & R camp on the lip of Kilauea Crater. There, in cabins once used by Japanese civilians interned, as at Utah's Topaz camp, as suspicious aliens, we luxuriated under our blankets while prisoner-of-war orderlies laid wood fires in our fireplace to take the chill off each new day.

Finally, in June 1946, the government realized it no longer needed me to help win a war, and I became once more a civilian. We spent the summer in Afton where I finally came to know, appreciate, and love Donna's parents. There, at the handles of a wheelbarrow, I helped lay the first sidewalks along many of Afton's streets, and am humbled to realize they will outlast anything material I accomplished in my subsequent career.

There, too, we experienced the mercy of a benevolent Providence. On a beautiful summer day Donna and I rode horseback seven miles up Swift Creek Canyon to Wyoming's unique phenomenon: the only intermittent cold-water geyser known in North America and one of only three—and the largest—known in the world. For 15-20 minutes water rises from a cavern deep in the mountain, overflows, then, drawn by a siphon effect, tumbles down the canyon to provide Afton the coldest, purest-tasting drinking water I have experienced. After 15-20 minutes the siphon is broken, the flow stops, and the cycle is repeated.

On this day, our idyll was cut short by a sudden thunderstorm sweeping over the mountain. With rain pelting down and lightning lashing the cliffs above, we galloped down the canyon. Seven months later our first child was born, having survived that wild ride during the most vulnerable time of his gestation.

Back at Reed College that fall, because of my previous INS experience I was able to get a job with the Northwest's preeminent newspaper, the *Oregonian*. I worked on the sports desk, generally twenty-five hours a week, helping cover prep and small-college sports and being responsible for ski coverage. That meant many weekends spent on Mt. Hood or other ski venues, providing welcome relief from the pressures of a full academic load. On one frigid night I joined the search for a skier lost somewhere on the six miles of trail running from Timberline Lodge down to Government Camp. As day broke we found him under a tree. His peaceful smile made me wonder if the last moments of death by freezing may be the most pleasant way to go.

During my final few weeks at the *Oregonian* I was moved from the sports desk to the city desk, just in time to help cover the biggest news story in the nation at that time. World War II crowded 140,000 defense workers into the Portland area, 92,000 of them in the three Kaiser Company shipyards. To accommodate them, Kaiser contracted to build the nation's largest wartime housing development. On 650 acres of Columbia River flood plain, near its confluence with the Willamette, quickly sprouted Oregon's second largest city. Named Vanport for its proximity to Portland and Vancouver, Washington, it contained 9,942 apartments, fourteen to a building, with shopping centers, a 750-seat movie theater, a 150-bed hospital, schools and day-care centers, and even the newly-established Vanport State College, which later, relocated, evolved into Portland State University. At its height 42,000 persons lived there, but ship-building slowed as the war wound down, and by three years after its end Vanport had shrunk to about 18,500.

On Memorial Day 1948, the Columbia River, swollen by heavy rains melting a near-record snowpack on much of its 260,000 square-mile watershed, breached the dikes protecting Vanport. Up to fifteen feet of water engulfed and totally destroyed the city. The official death toll was only fifteen, but for weeks after the disaster our coverage dealt with charges that officials had minimized the danger, had responded poorly—especially in relocating the nearly half of the population that was black—and had concealed a much higher death toll. The latter charge was never substantiated.

As Reed College graduation approached, I still intended to press on to a PhD in history and a career as a college professor. But shortly before Commencement Day, Albert E. Bowen, a Mormon apostle and chairman of the board of the Deseret News in Salt Lake City, came to Portland for a stake conference. Learning of my work at *Oregonian*, he invited me for an interview. The paper was expanding, he explained as he offered me a job.

To me, with an ulcer and occasional migraine headaches from the pressures of Reed's academic rigors combined with almost full-time employment, a year-long respite before the pressures of graduate study was tempting. I agreed to come for a year before going on to graduate school, but not at the salary he was offering. He raised it to the unprecedented starting salary of $300 a month. Based on a forty-hour work week, that is about $1.65 an hour. What 1948 college graduate could expect more than that? I accepted.

Corporal William B. Smart, 1944

Bill and brother Tom, 1944

Newlyweds-to-be: Donna and Bill in Portland, 1945

CHAPTER FIVE

Putting Down Roots in Zion

The day after graduation, we loaded our few belongings and our year-old son into a pre-war Nash, the first—and worst—car we ever owned, and headed for Salt Lake City. There we set up housekeeping in the basement apartment of a house at 60 South Eighth East. (It was razed some years later to accommodate the enlarged playing fields of Bryant Junior High School.) We showed up the next Sunday at the LDS Twelfth Ward, one of the first nineteen wards in Zion, established in 1849. There I soon received a calling that led to another of those unforeseeable events that profoundly changed and directed my life.

Leadership talent must have been in short supply in the Twelfth Ward, because two weeks after our arrival I was called to be leader of boys aged fourteen to sixteen in the ward's Explorer post and a teacher of the same age group in Sunday School. Some months later, I attended a training session conducted by a member of the general church Scouting committee. After listening impatiently for most of an hour to instruction in Boy Scouting, I interrupted to ask if we would soon get to Exploring. No, he replied, but the programs are similar. Even with my brief experience, I knew that was false, so I excused myself and left.

That bit of arrogance must have been reported back to headquarters. A few weeks later, I was called by newly installed superintendent Elbert R. Curtis to join the General Board of the LDS Church Young Men's Mutual Improvement Association. In prayerful consultation with Donna we concluded that Utah must be where we were intended to be, and the dream of graduate school leading to a quiet career teaching history on a college campus faded away. My planned year at the Deseret News turned out to be forty.

At age 27, I was the youngest member of the YMMIA board, along with Crawford R. Gates, born the same year and called to the board the same day. He had won fame by composing the 1947 pioneer centennial musical "Promised Valley," and went on to a distinguished career as a composer and symphony conductor.

When I arrived at the Deseret News, I became part of the paper's historic expansion. To prepare for it, a way had to be found to solve the critical post-war shortage of newsprint. Board chairman Albert E. Bowen found the way. In November 1947 he and general manager Mark E. Petersen, both apostles, partnered with Norman Chandler, publisher of the *Los Angeles Times*, to jointly purchase the Hawley Paper mill in Oregon City, including 13,000 acres of forest. The Deseret News paid 24 1/2 percent of the $8,500,000 price and owned that much of what became known as Publishers' Paper Company.

With newsprint assured, the *News* became for the first time in its history a seven-day paper, launching a 154-page Sunday edition on May 16, 1947. Along with a 24-page Farm, Home & Garden section, 28 tabloid-size pages of comics, and expanded sports, financial, art and music coverage, it featured a Sunday Magazine, locally written and edited, that became widely acclaimed in the next few years.

All this, together with more robust daily coverage, required greatly expanded staff talent. Feature writers and columnists recruited during this period became household names—people like Elaine Cannon, youth editor, whose column "Hi Tales" may have led to her later call as general president of the Young Women's Mutual Improvement Association; Winnifred Jardine, food editor; Hazel Moyle, garden; Evelyn Blood Sims, society; Howard Pearson, movies; Harold Lundstrom, chess and, later, music; Mabel Harmer, children's stories. Experienced newsmen were recruited from elsewhere—Ed Haroldsen, Palmer Chase, Bryce Anderson, Charles Wood. Despite the brevity of my *Oregonian* career, I was counted among them.

Wendell J. Ashton, whose history of the paper, *Voice in the West*, was published in 1950, was managing editor. L. Glen Snarr was city editor. Both men left in the 1950s for distinguished advertising careers. Both returned years later, Ashton as publisher, Snarr as chairman of the board. George Ford was Intermountain editor and soon built a staff of correspondents and far-spaced bureaus, from Boise to Idaho Falls to Grand Junction to Las Vegas.

The result of all this effort was spectacular. Circulation soared from 44,708 at the end of 1947 to 84,597 a year later. Advertising grew by 35 percent during that period. Classified advertising more than doubled.

My career at the Deseret News started July 1, 1948, on the sports desk, with a specific assignment to cover skiing. There was no waiting for snow. Three weeks later I was high on Mt. Timpanogos to assist with and cover a 24th of July ski race on the glacier (actually a permanent snow field) there. The racers were a hardy and enthusiastic bunch, hauling skis and slalom poles up the five-mile trail, with nearly 4,000 feet of elevation gain.

It turned out badly, though. By the time we reached the glacier, a heavy cloud cover limited visibility to a few feet. The slalom course was drastically shortened, but even then only a foolhardy few dared try it. The first of what I had planned would become the annual Deseret News 24th of July ski race was also the last. By the next summer I had been moved from sports to the city desk, and none of my ski editor successors ever attempted it.

Another innovation that first year lasted a bit longer. Under direction of the paper's promotion manager, Wilby Durham, we organized the Deseret News Free Ski School, with the legendary Alf Engen as head instructor and his brother Sverre and Olympic skier Jack Reddish his chief assistants. The first session convened on the slopes of Bonneville Golf Course on December 27, so these beginners could use their ski-related Christmas presents. Three or four hundred novice skiers were expected; nearly 2,000, mostly kids, showed up.

In an article written nearly 50 years later, the paper's outdoor editor, Ray Grass, wrote:

"They showed up on a cold, wintry day with every imaginable combination of ski gear...7-foot-tall skis held by 3-foot-tall skiers, rubber galoshes stuffed with newspapers to adjust fit, Dad's old leather ski boots, skis with no bindings, hands with no gloves, heads with no hats, bodies with no warm parkas."

"But, by golly, we taught them all," Alf Engen recalled. He

and his few instructors spent much of their time getting fallen skiers back on their feet and by the end of the day were exhausted.

The remaining four sessions that year were split between Alta and Brighton. They, along with other resorts, have hosted the ski school ever since. Until a few years before his death in 1997, Engen continued to direct it. Though a modest fee is now charged, it continues to put hundreds of youngsters on skis each year. In its more than 60-year history it may have introduced more beginners to skiing than any such program anywhere.

The Utah winter of 1948-49 was the fiercest of the century in the West, second in recorded history only to the winter of the "Great White Ruin" in 1889. Snowfall was near record levels. Temperatures in Salt Lake City were consistently the coldest ever, reaching 25 below zero in Salt Lake City and falling below zero two days in December, thirteen in January, and four in February. The yearly average of days below zero degrees is four. Other parts of the states were much colder. There was never a thaw; the snow just kept piling up. Blizzard after blizzard roared through the state, creating up to ten-foot drifts, closing highways, schools, and even rail lines, some of which were cleared with flame throwers. Three men died when a snowslide engulfed a train in Cache County. Ten others died from exposure in various places.

Aside from my newspaper duties, I was caught in a fierce personal battle with that winter. The basement apartment we rented was in the large two-story home of three elderly sisters named Manning. Rent was $60 a month, reduced by half if I would mow the lawn, rake the leaves and shovel the walks. That worked out fine in the summer and fall. But snow shoveling that winter was a vastly different matter. The driveway ran from the street to the rear of the house, then turned to serve a three-car garage. By mid-January I was carrying each shovelful of snow to throw it atop piles as high as my head. As the winter wore on it got worse; I had to climb halfway up the piles to deposit my shovelfuls. Among many unprofitable financial decisions I have made, that rent-saving deal was the worst.

In addition to covering skiing that winter, I found myself writing many of our weather stories. One of them could have cost my life. I noted a beacon light far out on Antelope Island, and wondered how they could keep it operating during a winter like this. The next day I called the Civil Aeronautics Authority and asked.

"One of our boys is going out for maintenance next week," I was told. "Why don't you go along and see for yourself? Dress warm and bring snowshoes or skis."

The "boy" turned out to be Harold Hardy, one of eight CAA maintenance technicians in Utah, each responsible for 250 miles of airway with ten to twenty beacons; Hardy had twenty. Each beacon was on a mountain-top somewhere, and each had to be serviced every month. "Along with many other duties, it's a big job," I wrote. "The man who fills it must be a plumber, electrician, carpenter, mountaineer, and truck driver." Also, in Hardy's case, a pilot; when the snow was too deep, he flew a ski-equipped plane to tend his beacons. And, on this particular day, it helped to be an arctic survivor.

Deseret News photographer Vern Dale and I met Hardy early the morning of Feb. 4, 1949. In an old four-wheel-drive Army ambulance we slushed through the frozen mud flats to the south end of Antelope Island and on to the adobe ranch house built in 1848 when the island held the Mormon tithing cattle. Now an historic site maintained as part of the Antelope Island State Park, it is the state's oldest Anglo house still on its original foundation. At the time of our visit it was still headquarters of a working ranch. There, the ranch hands served a memorable breakfast of lamb chops, eggs, and potatoes. We would soon need every unit of the calories it provided.

Tying skis behind our saddles, we set out to ride most of the length of the island. It was not easy. The snow was deep and swept level by the wind, hiding the snow-filled ravines and draws running down from the mountain. Frequently the horses would plunge in up to their shoulders, but with their experience would calmly back out and find another way. Finally, we tied up the horses, mounted our skis, and labored up the mountain to the beacon. We arrived in the dark and stumbled gratefully into a small shack. There, Hardy refueled the generator, checked the photo-cell that started it when the sun went down, and climbed a 65-foot tower to install a new 1000-watt lamp in the six-foot-diameter beacon.

By then, the wind was howling, the temperature below zero and the wind-chill far worse. I argued we should stay in the shack until morning. But Hardy, as his name suggested, was made of sterner stuff. He was anxious to get home, so we started. We would ski down the mountain as far as we could see when the rotating light was on our side, then wait, shivering in the dark, until it returned. Back at the horses, we numbly tied on the skis, mounted and let the horses pick their way home. The night was black, the wind tore at us, the cold was fierce. I seriously wondered if we would make it, and had some earnest conversation with my Maker about it.

After somewhat less than an hour, Hardy called a halt. "We have to get off and walk," he announced. "If we don't we'll freeze to death." Dale was too numb to realize the danger, and we had to physically pull him off his horse. Then it was walk to near-exhaustion in the deep snow and through the gullies, then ride, then walk, then ride, then walk, through the longest night I have ever known. Finally, we heard a dog bark in the distance—the most beautiful sound I have ever heard. Soon a lantern appeared, and we knew we were safe.

We virtually fell off our horses into the arms of the ranch hands, who hustled us inside to a roaring fire, hot drinks and food. In a tub of snow mixed with kerosene, our new friends gently rubbed our feet back to painful life. The ordeal to service that beacon had taken twenty hours. Modern navigation technology now guides airliners over or around the mountains.

The beacons have long since disappeared, which to my mind is just as well.

There were other stories I covered that terrible winter. Out in the western desert, sheep and cattle were starving and freezing to death, with ultimate loss reaching 25 percent. Back roads were choked high with drifted snow. Ranchers had no way to get feed to their herds and appealed for help to drop hay to them. President Truman and Congress allocated $750,000 to what became "Operation Haylift" in several western states. Utah's legislature added $250,000.

On one of the rare clear—but very cold—days I helped load a National Guard C-47 left over from World War II. With the Guardsmen I flew out to Skull Valley to drop hay to the herds stranded there and to tell our readers about rescue efforts. Flying at 150 to 200 feet, muffled and goggled and attached to the plane by safety lines, we opened the side cargo door and pushed out hay bales that burst upon landing and at least temporarily saved the lives of any cows strong enough to get there. That flight was one of many that saved thousands of livestock and the livelihoods of the ranchers.

Or there was the day I joined and wrote about a Snowcat expedition to take food and supplies to families stranded for days by snowdrifts burying the roads to the community of Granite, below the mouth of Little Cottonwood Canyon. It was that kind of winter.

Stories like these won a transfer from sports to the City Desk in the summer of 1949. There I was assigned to what was called rewrite, a position that involves receiving facts on breaking news stories phoned in by beat reporters and weaving them into a story worthy of publication. On a major event the rewrite man might receive information from any number of reporters and other sources. His is the first responsibility, often under stressful deadline pressure, to ensure that the resulting story is readable, accurate, based on credible sources, balanced, and fair. Behind him, the ultimate responsibility is the editor's. Maxine Martz, a veteran journalist and excellent writer for whom I had great admiration, filled the other rewrite spot.

Often, the rewrite person is assigned to work up a story on his own. One such, in the early months of my new position, drew national attention. In late January 1950, two Mormon missionaries, Stanley Abbott and Alden Johnson, disappeared in Czechoslovakia. For eleven days nothing could be learned about them other than that they had been trying to visit a Church member in a remote area. Finally, the Communist government, which had won power in a coup two years earlier, disclosed that they had been arrested for spying.

Negotiations brought an agreement; they would be released if they could be on a plane out of the country in two hours with all other missionaries following soon after. My all-night telephone vigil resulted in an interview with mission president Wallace Toronto and the first story announcing that the two missionaries were free and describing conditions of their captivity.

In addition to rewrite duties, I was assigned to do background and feature stories on the state's criminal justice system. The gloomy old state prison in Sugar House, with which I became very familiar, was deteriorating behind its fourteen-foot sandstone walls while a new prison was under construction at Point of the Mountain. Discipline and vigilance were deteriorating as well. Escapes were so frequent someone placed a sign on Twenty-first South in front of the prison: "Drive slow. Prisoners Escaping."

Among the criminal justice people with whom I became acquainted during this transition period was a parole officer named Hy Facer. He invited me to accompany him as he took a heroin-addicted convict for treatment at a federal drug treatment hospital in Texas. The poor fellow, in the throes of withdrawal, sat shackled in the back seat, moaning and sipping steadily on a bottle of paregoric to dull his agony and control his bodily functions. It was a long trip, because every hundred miles or so we had to stop for a fresh bottle of paregoric.

That journey, including interviews with the hospital's drug treatment staff, resulted in stories about the terrible human cost of addiction and the shockingly high rate of recidivism despite the lengthy and intensive treatment addicted patients received there.

It also resulted in my acquiring an addiction of my own. With our patient safely incarcerated at the hospital, on the way home we somehow wrestled our passenger car up a primitive jeep road into the spectacular area that would later become Arches National Park. It was my first look at Utah's red rock country. Years later, I resonated to Edward Abbey's description of that road and that landscape in his book *Desert Solitaire*:

> Leaving the headquarters area and the lights of Moab, I drove twelve miles farther north on the highway until I came to a dirt road on the right, where a small wooden sign pointed the way: Arches National Monument Eight Miles. I left the pavement and turned east.... Then another signboard: WARNING; QUICKSAND. DO NOT CROSS WASH WHEN WATER IS RUNNING.... The road, narrow and rocky, twisted sharply left and right, dipped in and out of tight ravines, climbing by degrees toward a summit.... Standing there, gaping at this monstrous and inhuman spectacle of rock and cloud and sky and space, I feel a ridiculous greed and possessiveness come over me. I want to know it all, possess it all, embrace the entire scene intimately, deeply, totally, as a man desires a beautiful woman.

Clearly, Abbey became hooked for life, as I had been.

Friendship with Hy Facer turned out to be exciting. On a sunny September afternoon in 1950 I left work and walked down Main Street to catch a bus ride home. At about First South I met Facer, and we walked along together. Near Second South he recognized a neatly-dressed man, greeted him with "Why hello, Bert," and took him by the arm. Thinking two old friends had met, I started to excuse myself. Before I finished, Bert smashed Facer with a right hand to the jaw, knocked him flat, and took off running.

Sensing this was a not entirely friendly act and that something might be wrong, I tackled Bert before he could get much of a start. We rolled around on the sidewalk in front of the Continental Bank Building, I chiefly concerned with holding his arms before he could reach a knife or perhaps a gun. Facer joined the melee, which greatly helped. A crowd quickly gathered, to whom Bert appealed, "Help! These guys are robbing me!" Fortunately, they didn't help him, but unfortunately, neither did they help us. After what seemed a long time, police arrived and hustled Bert into a patrol car.

This was well after the newspaper deadline, but I took time to call and alert our editors to the story I would be writing for the next day. Then I went to the police station to learn what this was all about. There I found Bert with his back to the wall, brandishing a chair to challenge several officers who, clubs in hand, were deciding what to do next.

"This won't help," I told him. "All this will do is get you beat up." "You think so?" he replied. Obviously relieved that he could back down without losing face, he submitted. Only then did I learn he was Bert Hall, a repeat offender and considered dangerous. He had escaped a few days earlier while serving time for his latest conviction of armed robbery.

Two postscripts: When I finally arrived home, Donna, frazzled by hours spent with a rambunctious three-year-old and a colicky two-month-old, demanded to know why I was so late. She stared in disbelief at my story that I had been busy catching an escaped convict and was not finally convinced until she read about it in the paper the next day. Shortly before Christmas that year, a package arrived from the prison. It contained a cowhide wallet from Bert, beautifully hand-tooled with my name, and a note thanking me. I still have it, but have never learned whether

42

it was a gift of genuine gratitude for saving him from a beating or a bit of jailhouse manipulation to win my support in a future parole hearing.

My final brush with the penal system was even more frightening. In early 1951, prisoners were transferred from the old Sugar House prison to the new one at the Point of the Mountain. They had been there only a few months when, on May 20, the most serious riot in the state's prison history to that time broke out. Instead of returning to their cells from the recreation yard, some 260 prisoners seized control of the main security building and took four prison guards as hostages. They vandalized the security building, breaking nearly every toilet bowl and wash basin; destroyed the electric control panels, leaving the facility without power; looted the hospital; and distributed narcotics among the rioters.

Governor J. Bracken Lee ordered the Utah Highway Patrol to take control. Highway patrolmen together with Salt Lake County sheriff deputies and policemen from Salt Lake City, Provo, Murray, and Orem surrounded the prison, armed with shotguns, sub-machine guns, and tear gas. But death row inmates, with nothing to lose, threatened to kill the hostages if any attempt was made to end the riot by force.

To break this impasse, the rioters asked to present their grievances to the media. Together with a reporter from the *Tribune*, I was chosen. Hearing the steel doors clang shut behind us as we entered that strife-torn place filled with angry convicts, many of them by then high on drugs, was not exactly nerve-calming. Facing the ringleader as he gently swung a menacing short length of chain with a huge padlock on the end didn't help. But the leaders presented their demands—chiefly dismissal of the deputy warden and captain of the guards—in a civil manner, and after fifteen minutes or so we were out of there. Satisfied they had made their point and that the public would read of their complaints, the convicts soon returned to their cells.

After the war, I had retained my status as an officer in the active Reserve, attending drills with units of the 96th Infantry Division at Fort Douglas. In 1951 my summertime tour of active duty was in the Pentagon with the Office of Chief Army Historian, doing research on the history of World War II. That summer I learned something of the intelligence and loyalty a dog can possess. By then we were living in the first home we owned, a small one at 1643 Harrison Avenue. In the backyard I had installed a doghouse where our English pointer Jeff slept. On the day I left for the Pentagon, on his own initiative Jeff began sleeping on the front porch. On the day I returned he went back to his doghouse.

Later that summer I was among 425,000 National Guardsmen and reservists called up for active duty in the Korean War. The examining doctors didn't diagnose the atrial septal defect with which I had been born. But they did discover the heart murmur it caused and placed me on inactive reserve, so I was spared combat in that war. It was just as well, for I was shortly launched into a new, more demanding phase of my career.

The sportswriter, 1948.

CHAPTER SIX

Shaping Opinions

From its 1850 founding in the tiny adobe mint building where the Joseph Smith Memorial Building now stands, the Deseret News moved four times before building its own home in 1926, a four-story brick building on Richards Street a few rods south of Temple Square. That's where I joined the staff.

It was a noisy place, exuding all the excitement and romance of newspapering in the days of hot lead type. The chattering of teletype machines filled the newsroom. Even noisier was the clacking of linotype machines in the composing room. Ours was a non-union plant, and the compositors had no objection when we writers joined them as they laid columns of lead type in the chase before locking up to print each page. Our task there was to help fit our stories into the designated space by cutting or eliminating lines of type as necessary. That required learning to read type backwards, a skill I have not entirely lost.

All that changed in 1952. Four years of intense competition for subscribers had bled both the Deseret News and the rival Salt Lake Tribune nearly white. In those days, John F. Fitzpatrick, long-time publisher of the Tribune, had become friends with LDS president David O. McKay, and the two along with Gus Backman, head of the Salt Lake City Chamber of Commerce, met frequently if not weekly for lunch at the Hotel Utah. It was said that many of the state's political, economic, and social issues were discussed and settled at those luncheons. It was probably at one or more of them that an agreement was reached to put the two newspapers into an operating agreement to save one or both from failure.

The resulting jointly owned Newspaper Agency Corporation

combined the mechanical, press, circulation, and advertising departments of the two newspapers. Advertisers were given a joint rate to appear in both papers. News and editorial operations remained separate and competitive. The contract was for a term of thirty years, assuring stability and profitability for that period.

But the Deseret News paid a heavy price. All its typesetting, composition and press work would be done in what had been the Tribune's but was now the NAC's production plant on Regent Street, nearly two of Salt Lake City's long blocks from our editorial offices. Editorial and newsroom employees were not welcome in that union plant. Until 1968, when the *News* built a gleaming new building on First South adjacent to the NAC plant, our staff labored with production inefficiencies that must have been unique in the profession. Where else was news and editorial copy tossed out a second-floor window to couriers who rushed it by bicycle or VW bug to linotype operators two blocks away? It didn't help that the great majority of NAC employees, from management down, had been Tribune people and were naturally oriented that way.

Far more damaging from a competitive standpoint, the agreement required the Deseret News to give up its cherished and highly successful Sunday paper. For the next thirty years, its subscribers would receive the *News* six days a week and the *Tribune* on Sunday. Producing a superior product despite those handicaps plus the natural advantages of a morning paper (the *Tribune*) over an afternoon one (the *News*) became the overriding challenge and passion of the Deseret News staff.

By then, my role in meeting that challenge had changed drastically. In early December 1951, less than four years out of college, I was reassigned to become an editorial writer on a three-man editorial page staff with me as the junior member. After only two weeks on the job, I learned that one essential for an editorial writer is a thick skin. The lesson came in a way that, even today, is hard to understand.

Elbert D. Thomas, an esteemed University of Utah professor of history and political science and a five-year mission president in Japan, had defeated five-term incumbent senator Reed Smoot in the 1932 election that also swept Franklin D. Roosevelt into the White House. In his eighteen years in the Senate, Thomas was a staunch supporter of the New Deal and was a leader, among other causes, in the struggle to convince the United States to assist Jews during the Holocaust.

In 1950, after the dirtiest political campaign in Utah history, he was defeated by Wallace F. Bennett. Though Bennett was never shown to be personally involved, his supporters conducted a whispering and pamphlet campaign falsely accusing Thomas of being pro-Communist or worse. In the poisonous atmosphere of McCarthyism, that was enough to defeat him, but there was more. Equally false rumors spread that he was an apostate, and the Law Observance and Enforcement Committee of Salt Lake County LDS stakes included him on a list of candidates considered unfit for office. It took a direct order from Church president George Albert Smith for the *Deseret News* to run a statement that the Church disavowed the list. That must have rankled Mark E. Petersen, an apostle who was also the paper's editor and general manager.

In December 1951 President Harry S. Truman appointed Thomas high commissioner of the U.S. Trust Territory of the Pacific Islands. It was a largely ceremonial position, given in recognition of his long service to the country. I recognized it as such and wrote a brief congratulatory editorial. On the evening the paper with that editorial hit the doorsteps, I was master of ceremonies at the annual Christmas dinner for the *Deseret News* staff. After dinner and a short program, I introduced Petersen to climax the evening with his annual Christmas message to the staff. The first part of his "message" was a scathing denunciation of me for writing and our editors for publishing such an editorial.

To me, this public outburst at such a festive occasion over a matter that could have been handled (if justified at all) with a private scolding, was deeply disturbing. Equally disturbing was this evidence of such bitter partisanship in the highest ranks of church leadership. Though I never failed to sustain Elder Petersen as an apostle, I never again felt really comfortable in my personal relationship with him.

Despite that rocky beginning, my status as junior on the editorial page staff did not last long. Our chief editorial writer was Vivian Meik, a distinguished-looking Britisher with a patch over an eye lost to German bombs in World War II. He claimed, as recorded in Wendell J. Ashton's Deseret News centennial history, *Voice in the West*, that he had graduated from Oxford and had escaped through enemy lines to Russia after defeat of the

British Expeditionary Force in its World War I Mesopotamia campaign; had worked as a railroad executive in Borneo, India, Manchuria, and central Africa, where, according to Ashton, he "walked every foot of the path traveled by Livingstone"; and that because of his work as a World War II correspondent, Mussolini had put a price on his head and Hitler listed him seventh among those to be executed when England fell.

All that may have been believable. Less so was his claim that when he joined the LDS Church he was granted lifetime exemption from Word of Wisdom standards. There was also concern about the occasional similarity of his frequent column, "Vivian Meik Says," to material previously published elsewhere. In any event, when increasing garnishment of his salary because of unpaid debts became intolerable, he was invited to leave the paper.

The second editorial writer was Sterling B. Talmage, son of the revered scholar, author and apostle James E. Talmage. He was brilliant, affable, and well-respected, but also aged. Shortly after Meik's departure, he retired, and in March 1952 I was suddenly, at age 29, editor of the editorial page. It was a position I would hold, along with later additional responsibilities, for the next twenty years. I quickly recruited John Talmage, Sterling's much younger brother and my frequent tennis partner or opponent, and Harold Lundstrom, who also became a close friend, as my associates.

Because of my youthfulness and inexperience, and perhaps because of my transgression with the Elbert Thomas editorial, I was required to run our editorials past J. Reuben Clark, former undersecretary of State and ambassador to Mexico, now second counselor to David O. McKay in the First Presidency. At day's end I would go to his home in the Avenues and there in his study, walls covered floor to ceiling with well-filled bookshelves, read each editorial aloud. He was then in his eighties, and I first thought his closed eyes meant he was asleep. I soon learned otherwise; he never seemed to miss a thing. I differed with some of his views, particularly his isolationism, but was discreet enough not to argue. After only a couple of months I had apparently gained enough of his confidence that pre-publication review at the General Authority level was no longer required, then or later.

As my own confidence and experience grew, I tried to follow

my conviction that building an effective editorial voice requires writing about issues that matter, that are debatable and debated, where an editorial position can have an influence. In the trade at that time we used a word—Afghanistanism—to describe writing about affairs that are remote, have little effect on our lives, and that our readers know little and care less about. How ironic that many years later, one of the most determinant, hotly debated, frequently editorialized issue of our times has been the longest war in our history, fought in Afghanistan and Iraq.

Taking a position on things people care about and that influences their lives is risky. People and organizations can bite back, and the writer had better be prepared to defend his position. That requires careful research and thoughtful analysis.

From early in my career as editorial page editor, I endeavored to expand the influence of that page beyond just the thinking of those who read it. The first major attempt to do so was one of which I am anything but proud.

Through the early 1950s, a controversy raged (and still does) over how the water of Colorado River Basin was to be used. The Colorado River Compact of 1920 guaranteed annual delivery of 7,5000,000 acre-feet of water to the lower Basin states, California and Nevada. The Upper Basin states, Utah, Wyoming Colorado, Arizona, and New Mexico, could divide up a like amount. But there was no way to use it without dams and reservoirs in the Upper Basin states. On the principle of "use it or lose it," those states united behind the proposed Upper Colorado River Storage Project to build dams on Colorado River tributaries throughout the region. A dam on the Green River in Utah's Echo Park was to be a key one.

In those days, there was little consciousness of the environmental and social costs of dam-building. Opposition was muted, except for the dam in Echo Park, which would flood particularly beautiful canyon country. Worse, it would invade Dinosaur National Monument, setting a precedent of violating national parks and monuments, which many thought unthinkable. David Brower, founding president of the Sierra Club, and Bernard deVoto, from his "Easy Chair" column in *Harpers Magazine*, raised powerful voices in opposition. They were backed by money and political muscle from an already-thirsty California opposed to anything that might deprive them of future additional water.

With all the vigor I could muster, but with little understanding of what I was writing about, I joined the fray with a series of editorials arguing the need for water development in the thirsty West. In one editorial urging a dam in Echo Park, I ridiculed Brower's rhapsody over the beauty of what to me were just rocks, and I debunked his excitement that wild geese floated down the river ahead of their rafts. Anyone who knew the wariness of wild geese would never write such nonsense, I pontificated.

L. Glen Snarr, city editor when I joined the Deseret News but now a senior officer in the powerful David W. Evans Advertising Agency, was lead lobbyist for the Colorado River project. He provided material, I wrote the editorials, and he mailed them out to Congressmen and, with my personal letter, to influential editors, many of whom I knew from conventions of the National Conference of Editorial Writers.

How much that influenced the outcome I will never know, but a letter in my files from Frank B. Woodford, chief editorial writer for the *Detroit Free Press*, gives an indication. He enclosed a column declaring that "because of my good friend Bill Smart I'm up to my neck in the Colorado River." Although he had never seen the river and didn't expect to, he wrote, he now supported the project.

In 1956, an agreement was reached to delete the Echo Park dam and build one in Glen Canyon instead. We supported that compromise, as did Brower and his Sierra Club, and Congress passed the Upper Colorado River Storage Act; the flooding of Glen Canyon became inevitable. To celebrate, the Evans Advertising people put together a three-day float trip down the Yampa and Green Rivers, where I began a love affair with the running of western rivers. The shame I felt as I experienced the majestic beauty and saw that wild geese did indeed accompany rafts down the river began for me a time of repentance that led to a new and different environmental ethic. Like Brower, I was soon to realize that supporting the trading of Echo Park for Glen Canyon was my worst ever editorial blunder.

The enormity of that blunder became clear to me when I experienced Glen Canyon the first of many times. By 1961, with Glen Canyon Dam two years from completion, Secretary of Interior Stewart Udall realized that at full flood what would become Lake Powell would invade Rainbow Bridge National

Monument and perhaps endanger the bridge itself. He invited me to join a small party to study how best to protect it.

I had become acquainted with Udall when he as an Arizona attorney and the Deseret News were independently working to expose the government's culpability in lying about the risks of its nuclear testing at Yucca Flat in Nevada, particularly the blast called "Dirty Harry" that in 1953 killed thousands of sheep and sent a deadly radioactive cloud over St. George. We shared information and developed mutual respect that ripened into a treasured friendship.

As for the Rainbow Bridge problem, there were three options. One was to limit the height of the reservoir to a level just below the boundary of the national monument, which would reduce both the reservoir's storage capacity and electric power production by the dam's turbines. A second option was to build a coffer dam below the monument, a small dam above, and a tunnel through the cliffs to divert Bridge Creek around the monument and into the reservoir. A third was to let the water rise and hope for the best.

Our study group helicoptered into Forbidding Canyon, hiked up to the bridge, and stood in awe of its majesty. We then decided to climb up the western buttress and study the topography from the top. That was difficult and frightening, made possible only by cables bolted into the sandstone at the worst spots. These were later removed after the Park Service made the climb illegal.

Only three of us, Udall, Brower, and I, made it. For more than an hour I sat atop the bridge with those two giants of western conservation, studying the landscape, marveling at its beauty, and philosophizing about the critical need to protect this magnificent country, not only here but throughout the Colorado Plateau. Their passion and breadth of knowledge and experience profoundly affected my future.

As for the three options to protect the bridge, we all agreed. Limiting the height of the reservoir was politically impossible; the water and power lobby was far too strong. Building two dams and a tunnel to keep the water out would irretrievably destroy the beauty and sanctity of the place. So the water was allowed to rise. At its maximum height it stood several feet in the channel below the bridge. But it never threatened the integrity of the bridge itself by reaching its buttresses. And as it receded, as it inevitably will continue to do long-term, floods down Bridge Creek scoured out the mud it left behind, leaving the cobblestones below the bridge as clean and shiny as before.

Another effort to expand the outreach of our editorials ultimately failed, but at least I can feel pride in having attempted it. The decade of the 1950s was an uneasy one. Our fears of a domino effect from a communist takeover of Korea had led us into an inconclusive war that cost 58,000 American lives without ending the threat, and it now seemed to be leading us toward the same kind of involvement in Vietnam. Efforts to reach nuclear weapons control failed, the Cold War continued, and the threat of nuclear war seemed real. Senator Joe McCarthy had been discredited and censured, but paranoia about communism still lingered, as evidenced by creation of the John Birch Society in 1958.

In that year I wrote a series of editorials under the general title, "Which Way to Peace?" The common thread was a call upon the nation to mobilize its spiritual and moral strength for peace. We called for President Eisenhower to create a top-level commission with as much strength and authority as the Hoover Commission to search out every possible approach to peace. We reprinted the editorials in a pamphlet mailed to key members of the administration, to all members of Congress, and to editors throughout the country.

As a fellow editor of a faith-oriented newspaper, I had become well acquainted with Roscoe Drummond of the *Christian Science Monitor*. In his nationally syndicated column he wrote "We have made tremendous efforts in international affairs without achieving the results we seek. Something new needs to be added to American foreign affairs.... In a continuing series of editorials, the *Deseret News* of Salt Lake City, a newspaper of deep spiritual conviction, has been advocating this course of action [creation of a Peace Commission] and it seems to me that it has been making a constructive case, and its voice should be heeded."

Sen. Mike Mansfield (D-Montana) spoke on the Senate floor: "Our nation's frantic race to build the perfect missile emphasizes the fact that we will only destroy ourselves unless we match our efforts for physical power with spiritual and moral strength. It is my opinion that the editorials carried in the Deseret News of Salt Lake City are well worth the attention of the Senate." At his request, these editorials were printed in the Congressional

Record on June 20, 1958: "The Practical Approach to Peace," "Let's Mobilize Our Morality," "We Need More Than Missiles," "Needed: Defenders of the Spirit," and "We Need Better Human Relations."

All that was gratifying, but more heartening to me was evidence of approval of the most skeptical of all audiences—the college generation. The University of Utah's *Daily Chronicle* editorialized: "Once in a while a newspaper other than our own accomplishes a journalistic feat of such excellence that, despite our own 'professional rivalry,' we must acknowledge such an accomplishment. Such acknowledgment must be paid to the *Deseret News* for its editorial page in the January 4 edition...We congratulate the writer of the lead editorial, 'Let's Mobilize Our Morality.'"

President Eisenhower was not impressed, not by a senior senator, nor a national columnist, nor even by a college editorial writer. When at his press conference a reporter asked his opinion about creating a Presidential Peace Commission his response was brief and to the point: "I don't think it would be useful at this time."

Still another outreach effort lasted much longer, was more effective, and almost launched me into a political career. In January 1958, the University of Utah's new public television station, KUED Channel 7, aired its first broadcast from a makeshift studio in what had been a cafeteria in the basement of the old student union building, today known as Gardner Hall. For some time I had been picking up a few dollars by acting as facilitator with Great Books discussion groups. Now, I proposed a unique project: Why not combine the Great Books discussion group idea with the resources of KUED and the op ed page of the *Deseret News* in a weekly program on public affairs? The concept quickly became reality. Civic Dialogue became KUED's first public affairs offering and continues today as Utah's second longest-running broadcast program, behind only the Tabernacle Choir.

The format was ambitious. We would choose an issue. If it was a local one, I or a staff specialist would write an op ed background article; if national, we would reprint an appropriate one or write our own. Discussion groups or individuals were urged to read these then tune to Channel 7 for an in-depth analysis by knowledgeable guests. Initially, the telecasts were two hours, the second hour devoted to questions or comments from the studio audience or phoned in by listeners. After a couple of years we simplified to one hour, still with audience participation.

We quickly realized that Civic Dialogue was an ideal format for political debates, and we hosted the first televised debates held in Utah. In an early debate I moderated in 1962, Rep. David S. King was challenging Wallace F. Bennett for his Senate seat. The basic issue was federal-state relationships. King, the Democrat, argued that the state could best move forward in active partnership with the federal government. Bennett, the Republican, called that "paternalism," and argued for self-help and limited government. King called that "obstructionism." How little things have changed today.

I moderated Civic Dialogue for nearly six years. Also during this period KSL-TV decided to air a weekly editorial, the first in Utah. They asked me to write it, which I did for the first couple of years.

Somehow, my journalistic activities during this period involved much more than writing editorials. They included several remarkable journeys. The first, in 1958, was to cover the dedication of the London Temple by President David O. McKay. Though we could hardly afford it, I determined to take Donna and to expand the itinerary to include much of Europe. As it turned out, that included an unintended trip into the heart of communist East Germany.

Kind friends offered to care for our children. Paul and Maureen Keller took our sons, age eleven and four, Brent and Helen Goates our daughters, age eight and six. A 15-month-old son was more of a problem. A worried but game Roy Darley, assistant Tabernacle organist, agreed to hand him to my parents at the Portland airport en route to a concert tour in Alaska.

Realizing now how much could have gone wrong, I wonder how we could have risked it. But we were young and more confident than wise.

The dedication of this first temple in the British Isles was a spiritual high that strengthened and energized the work there. One lasting physical memento resulted as well. On the temple grounds stood a noble oak tree, which President McKay had ordered preserved at all costs. Someone had mounted a plaque naming it the David O. McKay Oak. Our photographer, J M Heslop, took a picture. We enlarged it, had our artists place in the limbs photos of all his descendants, framed it, and presented it to him on his birthday. Years later, long after his death, during a tour of the historic McKay home in Huntsville, I was gratified to see the family tree prominently hung.

The London Temple is actually in the small village of East Grinstead, thirty miles south of the city. There we stayed in a sixteenth-century inn whose slanting and mismatched floors evidenced its age. On a free day, with Heslop and his father, we toured north to Oxford and Stratford-upon-Avon. Returning after dark, we managed to get lost in the maze of small roads south of London and reached East Grinstead around midnight in a soaking rain. The inn was dark and locked. Pounding on the door failed to rouse anyone. Emboldened by the prospect of the four of us spending the night in that tiny British car, I jimmied a basement window, crawled through, stumbled around to find a light switch, and finally opened the door to my soaked fellow miscreants. To me, our misadventure was reminiscent of but thankfully less deadly than the one of which Alfred Noyes wrote:

The road was a ribbon of moonlight over the purple moor
And the highway man came riding – riding – riding
The highway man came riding, up to the old inn-door...
Over the cobbles he clattered and clashed in the dark inn-
    yard,
And he tapped with his whip on the shutters, but all was
    locked and barred...

Apostle Henry D. Moyle, to whom as a neighbor I was home teacher, hosted a dinner at London's storied Claridge Hotel honoring President McKay's 85th birthday. During the day we had visited Windsor Castle, where I picked up and put in my raincoat pocket as a souvenir a small piece of the frieze that had fallen during a restoration. When we emerged from the dinner, I couldn't understand why someone had stolen my souvenir. A year later, Harold Bennett, CEO of ZCMI, and I left a dinner at Hotel Utah together. As we donned our identical raincoats, we realized they had been mixed up in London. "That explains it," Bennett said. "I never could understand why my coat had a pocket full of sand."

Following the dedication, Apostle Henry D. Moyle invited us to accompany him to an LDS district conference in Leipzig, deep inside Communist-ruled East Germany. It would be the first such visit by an LDS general authority since before World War II. The car carrying him was full, so we took the train. As we rolled through the ruins of East Berlin and on past empty farmyards and looted towns, we realized we had informed no one that we were going; if we disappeared, who would know?

Travel within East Germany was forbidden without a hard-to-get permit. But this was the time of the annual Leipzig Messe (Fair), to which travel was permitted. So the faithful Mormons came, nearly two hundred of them, in a few ancient cars, many more on motorbikes, by train or bus or on foot. We met in a partially bombed-out building. Apprehension was thick; travel was supposed to be to the Messe, not a church meeting. Would the secret police break up the meeting, or worse? But never have we felt a stronger spirit or more courage and faith. Never have we heard the songs of Zion sung with such energy. Never can we forget the tears we shed as in German they sang, "Sunshine in My Soul Today," including the words, "Jesus listening can hear the songs I cannot sing."

Following the meeting, I visited with the district president. What's it like, living under communism? I asked. His biggest concern, he said, was for his children. A daughter in grade school had been brought to stand before the class while the teacher led the students in jeering anyone stupid enough to believe in God. Why don't you get away, bring them to America? I asked. His response spoke volumes: "I can't. Our leaders have asked me to stay here, hold the Church together." Three years later the Berlin Wall went up, and escape was not an option.

The second of my three journeys took me to stand at the very bottom of the earth. In 1961, an invitation came from the National Science Foundation to study and write about the scientific research being done in Antarctica. A *National Geographic* writer/photographer and I were the only American journalists on the trip. Others were from Britain, Norway, German, and New Zealand. The seventh member of our small group was an elderly scientist who had wintered-over with Admiral Byrd at Little America in 1934.

Why did I receive such an invitation? It could only have been because a year earlier, at a reception of the National Conference of Editorial Writers in Washington, I had a conversation with an NSF official expressing interest in our Antarctic research since the International Geophysical Year of 1956-57.

In late November 1961, we flew aboard a Super G Constellation four-propeller Navy plane to Christ Church, New Zealand, with refueling stops in Hawaii and Fiji. Two days of briefings and issuance of arctic gear, and it was on to America's Scott Base on McMurdo Sound on the Antarctic coast.

For three weeks we lived among the scientists and described for our readers their work in the vast laboratory that is Antarctica. We walked arms-length from giant elephant seals and through a vast emperor penguin rookery where I held in my arms a chick still in its baby down but already weighing probably thirty pounds. We traveled by helicopter, ski-equipped plane, tracked Arctic Cat, dogsled, and an icebreaker. On the latter I learned that an icebreaker breaks really thick ice not by plowing through it but by running its spoon-shaped hull on top of it and crushing it under the ship's weight.

The icebreaker's current task was to carve a path through the Ross ice shelf to bring as close as possible a ship bearing Antarctica's first nuclear reactor to provide heat and power. Five miles offshore, eighteen crates weighing 30,000 pounds apiece were being unloaded. From there they were hauled by tractor sledges across the ice and halfway up Observation Hill to the plant site. Cost of the project, five million dollars, would be recovered within five years by saving the enormous cost of hauling diesel fuel to Antarctica.

In stark contrast to that modern technology, half a mile away stands a lonely hut, filled nearly to the rafters with long-drifted snow. It was built in 1902 by Robert F. Scott when he and his party, including Ernest Shackleton, trekked 380 miles south in the first real penetration of the continent. Six years later Shackleton and his party returned to this hut and safety after the specter of starvation forced them to turn back only 97 miles from the South Pole. In 1911, Scott and his party again set out for the Pole from this hut. Five of them reached it January 17, 1912, only to find that the Norwegian Roald Amundsen had been there a month earlier. All five froze or starved to death on the return, Scott and two others when trapped by a blizzard in their sleeping bags only eleven miles from a supply cache. In that hut, finally, ten members of Shackleton's 1914-17 party lived two years on seal meat after a blizzard blew their ship out to sea. Evidence of all that was still there, empty supply canisters, worn boots, a woolen mitten, canvas bags, uncounted seal skins, even a sheep carcass hanging from a rafter, no doubt brought by the relief party.

The heroism and suffering of those men left me with a sense of guilt as aboard a ski-equipped C-130 Hercules it took three hours to fly the 825 miles over which Scott struggled 77 days to reach the Pole. There we found the Scott-Amundsen research station atop two miles of ice but buried under drifted snow, both facts hard to comprehend since the polar plateau is one of the driest places on earth, with less than five inches of annual precipitation. Scientists there were researching upper-atmosphere physics, meteorology, glaciology, and, by studying each other in such harsh conditions, bio-medicine. With six months of darkness, the place also proved an ideal site for astronomy.

A pole flying a wind-whipped American flag stands exactly at the South Pole. I walked around it three times and have since dropped into casual conversation the remark that I have walked three times around the earth. I also mailed to family, friends, and people the Deseret News wanted to impress a Christmas card prepared by our artists, each bearing the postmark of the South Pole post office. Back home, I prepared a lecture featuring 2 1/4 x 2 1/4 slides from my Rolleiflex camera and presented it countless times.

The Antarctic experience led to another brief but unforgettable one. In 1958 the legendary Sir Edmund Hillary, whose 1952 first ascent of Mt. Everest thrilled the world, participated in the first crossing of Antarctica. From Scott Base he laid supply depots all the way to the Pole, to be used by Sir Vivian Fuchs coming from the Weddell Sea on the other side. In 1962, not long after my return from Antarctica, Hillary came to Salt Lake City on a lecture tour. We met and talked of Antarctica, particularly the awe we both felt about the hut that Scott built.

I asked how I could make his brief visit to Utah more enjoyable. He would love to get some exercise, he said, adding that he played squash. I had played competitive squash at college and still played regularly at the old Deseret Gym, so we went there. After a long, grueling point in the second game, he leaned up against the wall, gasping for breath.

"For a guy who climbed Everest, you're not in very good shape," I joked. "It's not that," he panted. "It's the altitude."

The third trip was even more ambitious, with lasting and far-reaching results. For years, Utah State University had enjoyed exchange programs and some lucrative contracts with Iran. The 1979 overthrow of the Shah ended those, and USU President Darryl Chase sought to explore places to replace them. He invited me to accompany him on a tour throughout South America. The idea was that his access to academicians and my access to government officials, through press credentials, would open many doors. Dr. Austin Hawes, a USU professor who, beginning with an LDS mission, had spent much time in Latin America, went along as interpreter.

For six weeks in 1962-63, including Christmas, we visited every country except Guyana, Suriname, and French Guiana on the north coast. My stories about countries and interviews with their political leaders were not particularly notable. More interesting, to me at least, were human interest and *Church News* stories we encountered on the way. Several events, people, and places stand out in memory.

One was a baptism in the Pacific off Vina del Mar, Chile. I wanted to photograph it looking back toward shore, so I backed into deeper water. A wave knocked me off my feet and wrecked my camera and the film in it.

Another was marveling at the ruins on my first visit to Cuzco, where in a Catholic church built on those magnificent Inca-carved stones is an early painting of the Last Supper with a fat guinea pig, his feet in the air, featured as the main course. Or in Machu Picchu, where diminutive, now-nearly extinct vicunas wandered with alpacas and llamas on the grassy terraces between the ruins. I proudly took home to Donna a vicuna cape, which, with her love of and sympathy toward animals, she refused to wear.

There was the Christmas Eve and Day spent in the palatial Lima home of a beloved aunt's brother, where I knelt with my hosts before their life-size permanent shrine and felt the depth of their reverence.

There was the drive on what television has since called the deadliest road in the world, from La Paz, Bolivia, over the spine of the Andes into the headwaters of the Amazon drainage. Where buses whizz on the narrow road around blind curves above thousand-foot abysses, dozens of white crosses marked the deadly result. I cannot forget the jolt of fear when one barely missed us.

A fonder memory was the trip in a jitney bus from Asuncion,

Paraguay, on a red-dirt road 200 miles to the bank of the mighty Parana River. There, passengers scrambled down the steep bank and boarded an open boat with an outboard motor. The bus, with our luggage, rolled down as well and onto a raft similarly powered. Worry about our luggage matched worry about our lives as the two ancient crafts chugged across the river. Hours later, worry was forgotten as we wet our feet above one of the world's great waterfalls, Iguacu.

But the really important result of the South America trip began one night in Lima. Late into that night we sat with Jim Boren, deputy director of U.S. Agency for International Development (USAID) in Peru, discussing the ineffectiveness of our financial aid to Latin America. Two years earlier, in 1961, President Kennedy had established what he called the Alliance for Progress, pledging ten billion dollars of aid over the next decade. This was the program Boren was administering in Peru. The main problem, we agreed that night, was that too often our money was being poured into dictatorial regimes that the people detested and feared. Instead of alienating the people, was there not some way our aid could go directly to them?

In January 1963, not long after Boren gave to his superiors a report of our conversation, President Kennedy charged USAID and Boren to find a way. In March 1964 USAID announced creation of a program called Partners of the Alliance, which, long outliving its parent organization, would become the largest network of volunteers in the western hemisphere. Jim Boren was named to head it.

As he and his small staff set about creating people-to-people partnerships, one of his first calls was to me. In view of their similar mining and grazing economies, he asked, would I take the lead in organizing the first such partnership, a Utah partnership with Bolivia? I would and did, recruiting Royden Derrick, president of Western Steel and a future LDS General Authority, as founding chairman and Gary Neeleman, a journalist with long experience in Latin America, as secretary. We held an organizational meeting in April, and the Utah-Bolivian partnership was born.

By turn of the century, that partnership had built 110 schools on the altiplano. Those schools became community centers from which the partnership helped local Bolivians develop self-help projects for economic and social development. The program dug dozens of wells to provide clean water on the altiplano. It established fifty dental centers, where Utah volunteer dentists treated thousands of kids and many adults. Utah State University, involved in the kinds of programs Darryl Chase had established, provided much help, including the use of vehicles.

The influence of the Utah-Bolivia partnership extended far beyond this state and that country. In 1966, the National Association of the Partners of the Alliance (NAPA) was formed to shift control of the program from the government to the private sector. Royden Derrick became its first chairman. He was succeeded as Utah chairman and later as NAPA chairman by Gary Neeleman. Under their direction and that of their successors, the program mushroomed nationally. A 2004 report claimed that it touched more than 200,000 people that year, with the leveraged value of its many and diverse projects more than $100 million.

A Change at the Top

As a member of the paper's board of directors, Ernest L. Wilkinson, president of Brigham Young University, was appointed chairman of the editorial committee. He was a man of great energy and tenacity who took his responsibilities seriously, not to say aggressively. He seemed to read every page and brought to every committee meeting a folder full of tearsheets, liberally marked with red pencil, and he did not hesitate to comment about them, usually negatively. His influence was widespread, and more than a few persons learned that he was not to be taken lightly, especially since he had the ear and support of then-aging LDS president David O. McKay.

One who learned was O. Preston Robinson, editor and general manager of the Deseret News since 1952, to whom I directly reported. Wilkinson's most frequent and harshest criticism was our carrying of Drew Pearson's column "Washington Merry-go-Round," which then ran in 650 U.S. newspapers, twice as many as any other columnist, with 60 million readers. Wilkinson insisted we cancel it. I argued that it made a valuable contribution by acting as a watchdog on government. Moreover, if we dropped it the Tribune would pick it up in a heartbeat and we would be seriously injured.

"Pres" Robinson, for whom I had great respect as well as affection, backed me all the way. It cost him his job. Though there was no hint of it publicly, I have never doubted that

Wilkinson's access to President McKay led to use of the Church's smooth and painless way of solving perceived personnel problems—a call to be a mission president. In this case, Robinson was called in 1964 to preside over the British mission. Years later, Wendell J. Ashton would leave by the same route.

Robinson had been grooming me as his likely successor, appointing me in 1962 his administrative assistant in addition to my editorial page duties, so I felt my time had come. But when he left for England, E. Earl Hawkes, a Mormon who was business manager of the *Boston Herald*, was chosen instead.

About this time, Congressman Sherman P. Lloyd, my distant cousin and good friend, decided to challenge Senator Wallace F. Bennett in the 1964 election. He urged me to run for the Republican House seat he was leaving. Others, because of my work on the editorial page or, more likely, my exposure as host of Civic Dialogue, had urged me to get into politics. Perhaps I was unduly influenced by one listener's telephoned comment during a political debate: "I'm not impressed by either candidate, but I'd vote for that guy in the middle." In any event, since my upward path at the Deseret News seemed blocked, and despite Donna's misgivings about being a political wife, we decided to make the plunge.

But again, our course was directed otherwise. On the first Sunday of February 1964, Sherman Lloyd and I found an empty classroom and spent a couple of hours discussing the complexities and strategies of running for his seat. On that very evening, Emigration Stake president Gerald Ericksen and his counselors came to our home and called me to be bishop of Federal Heights Ward. I was astonished. Our much-loved present bishop, George R. Hill, had served less than two years, and I felt that my service as chairman of the general Church Explorer committee was important. But Donna and I both felt the call meant this was where we were supposed to be. We accepted it and never again considered a political career.

Next to the choice of a marriage partner, it was the best decision of my life. As an editorial writer I had kept my party preference closely guarded and considered myself an Independent, but had I run it would have been as a Republican. 1964 was the year Barry Goldwater ran against incumbent Lyndon Johnson and dragged Republicans everywhere down to defeat. I too would have lost, would have been jobless and probably deeply in debt.

Instead, the next eight years gave expanding opportunities of leadership and preparation for future responsibilities.

Earl Hawkes proved to be a good fit for Deseret News leadership. He was affable, competent, courageous, and unfailingly supportive of his staff, especially me. I once heard him reply to a telephoning General Authority: "How can you say that about Bill when he's bishop of the most prestigious ward in the Church?" His entire newspaper career had been on the business rather than the news and editorial side, and he increasingly turned those duties over to me. In addition to overseeing the company's commercial printing operation, Hawkes turned much of his attention to community affairs. One of his many contributions was initiating the Christmas lighting of Temple Square.

Within a year of his arrival he made me executive editor over the news staff, and in 1968 expanded the title to executive editor and assistant general manager in addition to my title of editorial page editor.

An early and important decision during that period proved to be one of my best. Our *Church News* staff was struggling with dissension and poor morale. It needed new leadership, but who? I knew that of all our departments the photo department was the most harmonious, efficiently run. Why not make its head, chief photographer J M Heslop, *Church News* editor? To his astonishment and that of many others, we did. With his camera complementing the fine writing style he developed, and with the support and enthusiasm of a refurbished staff, the *Church News* flourished. Years later, I made him managing editor over the entire news staff.

Eight years of working harmoniously and enjoyably under Earl Hawkes ended suddenly and tragically. During our usual management meeting, August 13, 1971, he slumped over with what we thought was a heart attack. We rushed him to LDS Hospital, where they treated him for that. By the time they discovered the problem was rupture of an abdominal aorta aneurysm, it was too late. Dr. Russell Nelson, a friend from his Boston days, operated, but the small intestine, deprived of blood, had died. All he could do was clean out the ruined organs, knowing that death was inevitable.

Because intravenous feeding was substituted for the food Hawkes could no longer digest, death came slowly. For eleven months he lay in his hospital bed, tied to his tubes. For him it was the worst of times. For me it was not all that great. Responsibility without authority is hard, and that's what I had. Not only had I to run the paper, but to report daily to the man who was nominally still the editor. But the staff rallied, and I was proud of the paper we produced.

Mercifully for him, on July 24, 1972, this good friend died. But for nearly five more months my time in limbo went on. As days and weeks dragged on without me or anyone else being named editor, rumors spread that the paper was leaderless, riven with dissension, and foundering. The staff itself couldn't understand the delay, and morale suffered. Finally, in a memo to the chairman of the board, then-apostle Gordon B. Hinckley, I described how badly this indecision was hurting us, and declared that if I was not to be made editor someone else should be as quickly as possible.

On December 8, a Friday, N. Eldon Tanner of the First Presidency called me to his office and extended the invitation to serve as editor and general manager. He explained some of the reasons for the long delay.

One was President Harold B. Lee's irritation that I had opposed destruction of the Coalville Tabernacle. That impression, I responded, was no doubt because in 1966 I had been a founding director of the Utah Heritage Foundation, which did oppose it, but while I personally favored preserving the tabernacle I had never said so professionally or publicly. In fact, as a director I had been able to soften the foundation's criticism of the Church on this and a couple of other matters.

Another problem, Tanner indicated, had been my involvement in organizing the Friends of Church History. The irony of that made me inwardly gasp. Some months earlier, Leonard Arrington, the only professional historian ever to serve as Church Historian, had come to my office and asked me to become chairman of what would be the Friends of Church History. With too much on my plate already, I demurred. The First Presidency has approved the project, he said, and wants you to be chairman. Dutifully, I agreed.

At our organizing meeting we expected maybe a few dozen people. About five hundred showed up. Enthusiasm was high, and we collected membership fees. When nothing happened, after a few weeks I asked Arrington why. Apologetically, he explained that a single member of the Twelve had complained that the organization might encourage research by "Dialogue-type historians," so Friends was stillborn.

I was pretty sure that single member was Boyd K. Packer, who had famously preached that the proper role of a historian is to build testimonies, and that he had probably also objected to my appointment as editor. President Tanner said they had looked into the matter, found that I was "clean" and was "entirely free to lead that organization," which, despite having the approval of the First Presidency, no longer existed.

Unmentioned by either President Tanner or myself was what had to be the biggest elephant in the room. Ezra Taft Benson, a senior apostle, was an outspoken supporter of the John Birch Society, and that organization regarded me as a communist. Our two young daughters had been so informed when they visited a Birch Society booth at the state fair. The evidence was clear. I had been chairman of Utah's United Nations Day observance, and everyone knew what that meant. Moreover, I was a member of the Salt Lake Committee on Foreign Affairs and a founding member of the Utah Humanities Council, suspect organizations if there ever was one. The fact that I was being made editor anyway indicates how Benson's political views were regarded by his brethren. But I was under no illusion about my future as editor should he become president of the Church.

Editorial page editor

Civic Dialogue, with Sen. Wallace Bennett and David King, 1962; presenting David McKay's family tree to him, with Earl Hawkes

At the hut used by explorers at Cape Royds, Antarctica

With penguin chick

CHAPTER SEVEN

At the Helm

The thermometer stood at twelve below zero December 11, 1972, the day N. Eldon Tanner of the First Presidency and Apostle Gordon B. Hinckley, chairman of the Deseret News board of directors, announced to the staff my appointment as editor and general manager—sixteen months after I began performing those duties when Earl Hawkes was stricken.

Both expressed confidence in me, pledged the full support of the First Presidency, and asked from the staff its support and cooperation. I particularly appreciated this comment of President Tanner. "I don't know how you could have had a more difficult time than you've had since Earl took sick, to carry on as you have done, and I feel to congratulate you for the way you have done it and the way these people who are working with you have supported you in carrying their share of responsibility."

I began my response by recalling the prophecy of a senior staff member some months earlier: "It will be a cold day when they make you editor and general manager of the Deseret News." When the laughter subsided, I gave a brief statement of my feelings and goals. As recorded by my secretary:

> I don't propose to make a speech, but I do want to say a few things. First, I want from the bottom of my heart to thank you, my friends and fellow-workers, for the loyal and effective way you've followed through and done your work during these past months. As Elder Hinckley has indicated, they have been trying months with uncertainty, tension, and all of the production problems we have had. To the

68

department heads and to each one of you, I am so grateful for the professional, skillful way you have met your responsibilities.

Second, I want to express to Elder Hinckley, whom I love and who has been so much help and strength to me, to the board of directors and to President Tanner and the First Presidency, my appreciation for the trust and confidence they have placed in me.

Third, I'd like to say that I feel a debt of gratitude to two great men, Pres Robinson and Earl Hawkes. I had the wonderful opportunity of being at the side of each of them as they carried on these responsibilities. I have learned so much from them, and feel I'm privileged to stand on the shoulders of giants.

Now, where do we go from here? I say to President Tanner and Elder Hinckley, from here we go forward. We're going to grow. We're going to expand our influence in this broad area we serve. You know of some of the things we have planned to expand our outreach, and influence. I hope we can soon announce others. We're going to serve the entire community better than we have served them before. We are going to have more leadership in our community and in its affairs than we've had. We're going to provide a better paper, better editing. We're going to work hard on better, brighter, more interesting and readable writing. This is a challenge Elder Hinckley has given to us, and we accept that challenge. Especially, we are going to have honest, accurate, fast, courageous and professional reporting, the quality of reporting that will give this community the kind of newspaper it must have to fulfill its destiny in this great democratic society.

To accomplish these things, we are going to put aside any personal differences and work together as a team. I'm thrilled as I'm sure you are that George Ford will be the captain of that team as Managing Editor. He has done a great job under trying circumstances these past months. I know he has your respect and confidence and he certainly has mine, along with my gratitude.

That said, and in the years to come, our challenge was to

fulfill those promises of (1) excellence in writing, (2) leadership in the community, and (3), most important, quality, depth, and courage in our news coverage, so essential to becoming a first-rate newspaper. How we set about this challenging task is the subject of most of this chapter.

Excellence in Writing

As a first step in improving our writing, I installed assistant city editor DeAnne Evans as our writing instructor/watchdog. Bright, capable, respected and well-liked by the staff, but firm and demanding, she worked diligently with writers individually and in occasional workshops, liberally wielding a red pencil on offending copy—as did I. For emphasis on this goal, we established an annual awards dinner named for Mark E. Petersen, who spent most of his adult life at the Deseret News before and for a time after being called as an apostle. Awards were—and still are—given in several categories, but by far the most prestigious and coveted was and is the Excellence in Writing award.

Our next move was to adopt William Strunk's book *Elements of Style* as our writing bible. I gave a paperback copy of this little book to every staffer and new hire, with an admonition to study it carefully. If you want to remain at the Deseret News, I warned, you had better memorize his eleven "Elementary Rules of Usage." Then, when I spotted a rule violation—Its a wise dog that scratches it's own fleas (Rule 1); or Give it to my wife and I or to his wife and he (Rule 10); or the dangling participle: Being in a dilapidated condition, I was able to buy the house very cheap (Rule 11)—I simply scribbled on the copy the number of the violated rule, which sent the writer off to commune more deeply with his Strunk.

In making new hires and in evaluating present staff, I gave first priority to the quality—or what I sensed to be the potential quality—of their writing. Never having taken a journalism class myself, I paid little attention to degrees in journalism. I was more interested in the breadth of his or her education, especially in the humanities, social studies, literature, and the arts, studies to help them understand and interpret the human condition, with a solid foundation of ethics and values and critical thinking. Moreover, convinced that the surest way to become a good writer is to read good writing, I wanted to know what they were reading.

It's hard to measure the results of such emphasis, but I'm confident that, led by people like Don Woodward, Clifton Jolley, Carma Wadley, Doug Robinson, Elaine Jarvik and others, the quality of our staff's writing reached a level not seen before or, sadly, since. Partly, quality decline is due to modern production technology. Time was when copy went through a series of editors, headline writers, and even linotype operators, any of whom could catch and correct a grammatical or other error. Today a story can flow from the writer's computer onto the press without ever being carefully read. Editors often have no time for careful reading, and sometimes one gets the feeling they don't care. If newspapers suffer this disease, television is far worse, particularly, it seems, among sportscasters. Their misuse of proper pronouns seems endemic. How long will it be until a statement like, "The coach tried to explain to his fans and I why he called that play" becomes common and accepted usage?

Community Leadership

The newspaper's opportunity and responsibility to lead out in improving its community was something I had undertaken even before becoming editor in chief. As executive editor I initiated in 1969 the Deseret News Goals for Utah program. Each year we invited to a continental breakfast thirty or forty Utahns representing various interests and professions. We divided them into small groups to brainstorm goals they would like to see accomplished. We then published a list of their suggested goals and invited our readers to prioritize their top three choices.

On the basis of that input, the editors selected three or four goals to work on that year. Selected goals included things like improving public transit, establishing bike trails, better financing of public schools, and promotion of Utah skiing and tourism. Some were repeated for several years. Wherever feasible, we partnered with other interested organizations to achieve them.

On some goals, significant progress was made; on others, not so much. One on which progress has been measurable and impressive and continues to this day was to clean up the Jordan River and make it accessible for public enjoyment. In 1973 the legislature had created the Jordan River Parkway Authority, but without funding little had been done. To get things moving, we organized what became the Provo-Jordan River Trails Foundation, recruited a few interested and capable people to become a board of directors, and obtained tax-exempt status. Our vision, inspired by the beautiful urban river walkways of Boise and San Antonio, was a series of trails and parks from Vivian Park along the Provo River to Utah Lake, then forty miles along the Jordan River toward Great Salt Lake. After a couple of years of little action, I agreed to become chairman, and by putting the arm on affluent friends raised a few hundred dollars as seed money.

We needed a major fundraising event to jumpstart the project. Some board members urged the usual way—a gala dinner and auction. No, I said, this is an outdoor project; we need to be outdoors. And besides raising money, we need to raise public awareness and show legislators and community leaders what the river is—in many places a trash dump—and what it can be. So it was decided; our fundraiser would be a canoe excursion down the Jordan, ending with a barbecue.

We had great cooperation. The Salt Lake Boy Scout Council loaned the canoes. Salt Lake City parks people handled the launching, the takeout, and the barbecue. A string band provided western music. Granite Mills donated a small souvenir canoe paddle for each guest (for years, mine provided emergency power whenever my Hobie Cat sailboat was becalmed on Bear Lake).

To give the occasion a special flair, I felt that rather than beef we needed to serve buffalo. After partnering with Governor Scott Matheson in one of our weekly tennis matches, I asked him if a buffalo from the Antelope Island herd might be available. Shortly before we needed it, a side of buffalo was delivered. A local butcher processed it into steaks and buffalo burgers.

On a bright September afternoon in 1983, the largest flotilla of canoes yet seen on the Jordan launched from River Park at Seventeenth South, carrying fifty or so legislators, civic officials, and potential corporate or big individual donors downstream to a Riverside Park takeout at Tenth North and Redwood Road. That's only a little over three miles of river, but enough to show its deplorable condition and also to visualize that a walk, jog, or bike ride along or a canoe float down a cleaned up and accessible Jordan River as it flowed through a major city could be a delightful escape into nature.

After Frisbee golf, horseshoes, volleyball, a lot of laughter and accounts of near-capsizes and narrow escapes from overhanging branches, a spectacular meal was served. The speeches that followed were brief and to the point, and the guests left seemingly happy and supportive of the project. But the next morning the *Salt Lake Tribune* published what it considered an expose about a bunch of fat cats being able to get a buffalo from the sacrosanct Antelope Island herd. The governor's office did damage control by explaining that this buffalo was sick and had to be destroyed. That silenced the *Tribune*, but left us with a problem—how to convince these generous and in many cases distinguished donors that we really hadn't fed them sick buffalo. That took many one-on-one phone calls made more believable by the crucial fact that no one got sick.

Despite that somewhat duplicitous beginning, our strategy worked. Public awareness of the river's needs and potential had been raised, especially among decision-makers. We kept awareness alive with a series of articles and events, the legislature responded with funding, and by 1986 $18 million had been spent to acquire property and four miles of trail had actually been built. Today, a beautiful trail begins at Vivian Park in Provo Canyon and runs along the Provo River past Bridal Veil Falls and, with some detours, fifteen miles to Utah Lake. From there, it runs through Lehi, seven Salt Lake County communities, Salt Lake City, and on into Davis County, where it links with trails running all the way to Roy. In 2012, Salt Lake County voters approved a $46 million bond to complete, along with other projects, the four remaining unbuilt sections of the trail in the county. A total of 76 miles of paved Provo-Jordan River Trail through three counties welcomes runners, walkers, and even wheelchair riders, while canoes and kayaks cruise alongside. The trail runs through or beside five golf courses, wildlife preserves, an equestrian section, and numerous parks, including one for OHVs and motocross and one for flying radio-controlled airplanes—all of these built or established since those early-morning breakfasts helped identify this as a needed Goal for Utah.

The goal of promoting the Parkway led to an unusual Utah phenomenon though not in the Parkway itself. In 1984, as a College Commission member of the Northwest Association of Schools and Colleges, I was part of an accreditation team visit to a junior college in Valdez, Alaska. At this bustling town at the south end of the 800-mile Trans-Alaska Pipeline, I spotted a giant wooden Indian statue in the city park. It was carved with a chainsaw, I learned, by a strange man with a goal of creating such a statue in every state, charging nothing for his labor.

At that price, I concluded, Utah needed such a statue as a feature of the Parkway, probably to stand where North Temple crosses the Jordan River at the state fairgrounds. I contacted the artist, Peter "Wolf" Toth, a 37-year-old refugee from Hungary who had fled with his family when Soviet tanks crushed the 1956 Hungarian Revolt. In his mid-twenties he had become obsessed with honoring our Indian heritage by carving what he called his "Whispering Giants" in every state, and had worked on the project ever since.

Would he come to Utah and carve us a statue? I asked. "Sure," he responded. "All you need to do is find a huge tree and mount it on a suitable base."

Lynn Pett, superintendent of Murray's city parks (later its mayor) was an especially energetic and effective member of our Parkway board. He urged that a more prominent site for the statue would be on State Street at the entrance to his new Murray City Park. Since that meant he, not I, would have to find the tree and mount it on a base, I agreed. He found a giant cottonwood growing along the Jordan River near 4800 South.

Toth arrived in an ancient van containing his tools and sleeping bag. In nearly three months of magic with chainsaw and chisel, eating and sleeping at the site, he completed the task, then quietly slipped away to do his thing somewhere else. Chief Wasatch, twenty-three feet tall, still guards the entrance to Murray City Park, inviting all of us to remember and honor what the Ute, Shoshone, Goshute, Paiute, and Navajo peoples have contributed to the Utah culture.

Saving Westminster College

Membership on the NASC College Commission gave me an opportunity to make a far more important contribution, this one involving the survival of Westminster College. The school was founded by the Presbyterian Church in 1875 as part of an effort to wean children from Mormonism while they attended Protestant primary and secondary schools. In 1895 it became a college and in 1902 was renamed Westminster College. The Presbyterian Church ended its sponsorship in 1974, and the college began a slide toward bankruptcy. By 1979 it was $3.1

million in debt, with a $573,000 deficit projected for the coming year. Understandably, President Helmut Hoffman resigned.

In this crisis, Kennecott Copper loaned its industrial relations manager, James E. Petersen, to become acting president. This tough former miner and union leader, who had no college degree, was known for shutting down a Kennecott operation in Lark, effectually destroying his own hometown. R. Douglas Brackenridge records in his excellent history of the college that "gallows humor around the campus claimed that rather than a rescue mission, Petersen was coming to Westminster 'for a lark'."

It wasn't quite that bad at Westminster, but it was anything but a lark. He cut half a million dollars from the budget by eliminating nine full-time and many part-time faculty positions, reducing the administrative staff, cutting student and other services, and eliminating all intercollegiate sports. Realizing that the college would never prosper without Mormon support, he recruited two highly-respected but somewhat lapsed Mormons, Sterling McMurrin, former U.S. Commissioner of Education, and Obert C. Tanner, businessman and philanthropist, to obtain that support. They persuaded N. Eldon Tanner of the church First Presidency to become honorary chair of a $3 million fundaising campaign, which he started with a $100,000 contribution and a promise of more to come. After eight months of strenuous service, including raising a million dollars, Petersen returned to Kennecott.

But under the new president, C. David Cornell, conditions again deteriorated. Enrollment declined, debt grew, faculty morale plummeted, a major building (Ferry Hall) was condemned and others badly needed repair. A NASC College Commission accreditation team returned from its inspection visit in the fall of 1981 with a report that Westminster was on the verge of collapse. It recommended that accreditation be revoked.

That would have been a death blow to Westminster. The college needed a new administration, I argued, and a new one should be given a chance to succeed; let's grant accreditation but make it conditional. The Commission agreed. Its stern letter to Cornell set a deadline for needed improvements, warning that "The action is to be interpreted as a next to last chance for Westminster College to demonstrate that it continues to merit the confidence that accreditation implies." This was reported to the media in such a way that the college newspaper ran a story with the headline: "WE DID IT!" implying, as Brackenridge wrote, that the college had passed its accreditation inspection with flying colors.

Cornell resigned in January 1982, and Peterson was called again to the rescue, this time as permanent rather than acting president. The three and one-half years of his administration saw tough love in action. He cut faculty salaries to a level he called a disgrace but necessary, eliminated tenure and eight faculty positions, and rewrote the by-laws to assure board of trustees control of the college, free of faculty interference. All this was done without faculty input and with the blunt warning that any opposed faculty member should seek employment elsewhere.

Still the college struggled on the verge of fiscal collapse until, in 1983, Berenice Jewitt Bradshaw, widow of the murdered oil and auto-parts magnate Franklin Bradshaw, made the first of her gifts that two years later totaled more than $2 million. Wilbert (Bill) Gore of Gore-Tex became another major donor. Other individuals and foundations followed, and an October 1984 NCSC visit resulted in a report that the school had "recovered well and is now in a sound fiscal and academic condition."

Having presided over this remarkable turn-around, Petersen took well-earned retirement in 1985. Under successive presidents Charles H. Dick (1985-95), Peggy A. Stock (1995-2002), Michael S. Bassis (2002-2012), and Bryan Levin-Stankevich (2012-present), steady academic and financial progress has given Westminster, once so perilously close to failure and closure, today's ranking among the better private liberal arts colleges in the country.

Shaping Utah's Future

Deseret News leadership through Goals for Utah and other projects led to my involvement in a program that became, and still is, a major influence in shaping community development in Utah. In the late 1980s Utah was struggling with a flat economy, with people leaving the state to find jobs elsewhere. A few of us, self-appointed but concerned about the lack of long-range planning, gathered at the Pack Creek Ranch near Moab to brainstorm about what could be done.

For two days we vented our concerns: a governor and

legislators primarily concerned with the next election; no visionary thinking about what a future Utah should look like; no planning about how to get there; no cohesive force to accomplish it even if we knew. There was a lot of talk about the days when LDS president David O. McKay, *Tribune* publisher John Fitzpatrick, and Chamber of Commerce president Gus Backman met regularly for lunch at Hotel Utah. Decisions reached there about Utah issues and needed projects were seldom ignored by the governor or legislature. How could we replicate something like that?

After two days of discussion that seemed to get nowhere, I made a motion that we organize what we would call the Coalition for Utah's Future. No doubt relieved that something might come out of all this talk, the group unanimously agreed. None of us, certainly not me, had a clear vision of what the coalition would be, how it would operate, how it would be funded, or what it would eventually become. But I had long since learned that if we will just get started in a selfless way on a task that is worthy and important, providence will join in the effort. It's amazing how things fall into place, how help comes from unexpected places. So we set about getting started.

We organized the Coalition for Utah's Future in 1988, with a diverse board of community leaders, activists, academicians, business and media executives. I was made vice chairman. An early priority was to stage an event that would not only raise operating funds, but would also command public attention. I proposed we stage a gala dinner for corporate foundation and other potential donors, government officials and community leaders featuring an address by Wallace Stegner, who had long been a critic of exploitation of the West and an ardent spokesman for a brighter future. A TV documentary on Stegner's life had just been completed, and I proposed we use a portion of it as an introductory to his address.

Years earlier, when I was chairman of the LDS Church Explorer Committee, we had established a hiking trail for Explorers over the last and most difficult 36 miles of the pioneer trail, from Henefer to This is the Place monument in Salt Lake City. I researched and in 1958 wrote a pocket-sized guide to that part of the trail, and we had Explorer posts build monuments at important places along it. (The last remaining one is below Donner Hill just above the mouth of Emigration Canyon. In 2016, the plaque was long gone, and I raised funds to have it replaced.) When he was researching for his book on the epic Mormon exodus to the Great Basin, published in 1964, Stegner somehow learned about my involvement and called to ask if I would take him over those 36 miles. Trying not to sound too excited, I agreed.

We spent a glorious autumn day four-wheeling and hiking the trail, managing to get my battered green Blazer stuck in East Canyon Creek. Some of what he learned that day can be found on pages 203-24 of his classic book *The Gathering of Zion*, along with mention of it in his Acknowledgements. After all the books that have been written in the nearly half century since then about the Mormon exodus, his *Gathering* remains, in my opinion, by far the most readable and insightful.

Hoping he remembered that day together, I called Stegner, explained the purpose of our infant organization, and asked if he would come and help us get off to an enthusiastic start.

"Bill," he responded, "I'm in my eightieth year; I don't give talks anymore." That's understandable, I said, but could you come so we could introduce the documentary and honor you, then give a brief response? Graciously, he agreed.

After meeting at the airport, we spent much of an afternoon visiting his haunts of more than sixty years earlier, including East High, from which he graduated, and the University of Utah, where he had been a member of the tennis team.

Two things about the dinner meeting that night, besides the impressive gathering of business, community, and government leaders, stand out in memory. One, for both Donna and me, was sitting at table with Stegner and Robert Redford, listening to the interchange between these, to me, heroes of western conservation. The other came after the honor of introducing Stegner. Instead of a brief response, he delivered a moving twenty-five minute address, lauding the purpose of the Coalition for Utah's Future, describing the priceless heritage of our western lands, and pleading for that kind of vision to protect them for future generations. It may have been among his last such speeches; tragically, five years later, at age 84, he died after an auto accident.

That memorable launching of Coalition for Utah's Future led to corporate and foundation grants that, through the years, enabled a movement of present scope and outreach that none of us at that Pack Creek Ranch meeting could have envisioned. Early projects focused on affordable housing, education, rural economic development, water and air pollution, transportation, urban sprawl. Through contacts I had made on behalf of the Grand Canyon Trust, I was able to obtain a grant from the Hewlett Foundation, whose emphasis was on conflict resolution, to try to resolve conflicts over BLM wilderness. We focused on Emery County and the Waterpocket Fold but accomplished little; wilderness remains a bitterly unresolved issue.

Projections that population on both sides of the Wasatch from Brigham City to Nephi would soar from two million to five million by 2050 focused the Coalition's attention on planning for sustainable, livable urban growth. Stewart Grow became the energetic, effective chair of the Coalition's Quality Growth Steering Committee. That evolved in 1992 into what still functions as Envision Utah, with Grow at the head. He was followed by Jon Huntsman and other able leaders. Under its direction a series of workshops involving extensive public input produced a consensus for walkable, sustainable communities of homes, shops, office buildings, schools, trails, and parks. That is the pattern on which Kennecott's huge Daybreak community in South Jordan and smaller projects elsewhere have been built. Envision Utah, the outgrowth of that small gathering at Pack Creek ranch, is being replicated in Ogden, Provo, and St. George, and gives promise of continuing to be the major influence for smart growth in Utah's future.

It may also fill a key role in tackling another of Utah's most vexing problems, its dirty and unhealthy air. After years of much talk and little action, Gov. Gary Herbert in 2013 formed a 38-member task force to study and recommend a comprehensive program to clean the air. The effort will be organized and co-ordinated by Envision Utah, which, the governor said, "has set the standard for its collaborative leadership in defining the issues and engaging public participation in key policy arenas."

Other Projects

Other outreach efforts had less far-reaching and important results, but do continue to add to the richness of community life. The first after my appointment as editor and general manager was establishment of what became the annual Deseret News Art Heritage Show. My concept was to encourage emerging artists by giving their work exposure and recognition. Established experts juried the show, choosing six paintings for Awards of Merit. Winners that first year, 1973, were Dan Baxter, Paul Ellingson, Eugene Juhlin, William Parkinson, Gary Smith, and Edward Taggart, all little-known at the time, but most having gone on to successful careers. From the Award of Merit winners, Deseret News art director Charles Nickersen and I chose each year one for our Purchase Award, which also became the Deseret News Christmas card. Through the years these paintings have accumulated into a valuable corporate collection of Utah art.

We continued other programs that still make a contribution, including: Salute to Youth, an annual concert of young musicians with the Utah Symphony; Sterling Scholars, honoring outstanding high school students; Newspapers in the Classroom, incorporating use of the *Deseret News* into the middle school curriculum, the Deseret News Ski School, and others.

I had long made good use of the *World Almanac and Book of Facts*, and one day the idea hit me—why not publish a Church almanac? Our board of directors approved, and in 1974 the first volume appeared—ninety pages, entirely staff-produced. That was a big effort for a staff that had never done such a thing, and the next year we recruited the Church History and Archives as our partners. Through their knowledgeable efforts, the bi-annual *Deseret News Church Almanac* has grown to the 608 fact- and information-laden pages of the 2013 edition.

Three other projects, one of which continues today, had to do with running. In 1970, near the beginning of the running craze, Fred Holcomb, an avid runner fresh from the Boston Marathon, walked into my office with a proposal: why doesn't the Deseret News sponsor Utah's first marathon? He offered to organize it, along with Keith West, our promotions manager. So, in Utah's first marathon, some fifty runners started in Davis County and ran along old Highway 89, most of them to finish 26 miles later in Salt Lake City.

The next year we got smarter. We made it a Days of '47 marathon, following the Pioneer Trail down Big Mountain, over Little Mountain and down Emigration Canyon, finally down Main Street in front of the thousands gathered for the parade, with a finish at Liberty Park. Within a couple of years and for years after, still under West's direction, we had a thousand or more entries for what *Runners World* magazine called one of the top ten marathons in the country. After seven years of greeting runners at the finish line, I decided to join the party. In 1978, at age 56, I ran the first of four Deseret News marathons, but I was never very good. Only in the mostly downhill St. George marathon was I able to finish a marathon in under four hours.

The following year, 1979, we got even more ambitious about running, organizing a 1,450-mile relay from Nauvoo, Illinois, to Salt Lake City to celebrate designation of the Mormon Pioneer Trail as a national historic trail. From May 21 to June 1, except Sunday, more than 450 runners from all over the United States and from Canada and Mexico, all descendants of early pioneers, ran ten-mile segments night and day. Batons passed from runner to runner carried messages to LDS president Spencer W. Kimball from governors along the route.

After conducting a departure program in a Nauvoo riverside park, I crossed the Mississippi with two other runners in an open boat and ran the relay's first leg. A cold wind buffeted us as we reached Sugar Creek, seven miles from the river. I thought of the Saints driven from Nauvoo who huddled there in their tents in sub-zero February, where Eliza R. Snow reported nine babies born in those tents the night before she arrived, where the arrival of flocks of quail saved the half-frozen saints from starvation, where it took the arrival of Brigham Young, after ten days of waiting in the bitter cold, to raise flagging spirits and organize into companies for the long trek west. Remembering all that, I forgot the wind.

After the success of that relay, I conceived another, which we called the Deseret News Red and Blue Relay. On the day University of Utah and Brigham Young University met in their annual football rivalry, students of the two schools raced each other in relay teams from the idle stadium to the one packed with fans, entering shortly before kickoff. We ran it two years, once each way. When the second year brought less enthusiasm and participation than the first, we decided that was enough.

Newspaper editors are often asked to serve on various boards and in various causes. Some decline, in accordance with their paper's policy. Counseled by our owners to be as involved in community affairs as newspaper demands allowed, I generally accepted, though in some cases my contribution was little more than a name on the letterhead. Among those to which I did give time and energy, not named elsewhere in these pages, were the

Utah Constitutional Revision Commission, Utah Symphony board (special adviser to the president), Pioneer Theater board, Snowbird Institute board, Salt Lake Chamber of Commerce board, Friends of KUED board (chair), Bonneville Knife and Fork and Timpanogos clubs (president of both), the Western States Arts Foundation, Utah Humanities Council (founding board member), and the 1973 Olympic Bid Committee. On the latter, I agreed to serve mostly to give me opportunity to oppose bringing the Olympics here if it meant holding any part of them in Big or Little Cottonwood canyons. Fortunately, when they did come in 1992 those canyons were spared.

Shortly after becoming editor, I was inducted into the Alta Club, which is worth mentioning only as a commentary on Salt Lake City's social structure. Founded in 1883 by non-Mormons for non-Mormons, the club had been largely non-Mormon since then. N. Eldon Tanner, prominent businessman and first counselor in the First Presidency, and O. Preston Robinson, my predecessor as editor, had both been blackballed, I was told. Whether my admission was because Jack Gallivan, publisher of the *Tribune*, sponsored me or because I was a less-visible Mormon who might not be as offended as they would have been by the drinking, cigar smoking, and poker games going on there, I never knew. Women were of lesser status, even, than Mormons. Not until 1987 did the Alta Club take the momentous step of admitting women as members. And for decades, a woman could enter the club only through a side door and up a narrow staircase to the dining room.

A Newspaper to Make a Difference

Involvement and leadership in community affairs was important, but a more important and greater challenge in fulfilling our promise to President Tanner that cold day in December was to build a newspaper whose news and editorial columns demonstrated consistent quality, depth, and especially courage. What I had seen in my time there, and heard about from others, was a newspaper that sailed placidly along, reporting the news routinely but making few waves and not going deep enough to discover what caused those that did appear. I saw little of what I believe is the role of a newspaper, as the saying goes: to comfort the afflicted and afflict the comfortable.

This is not to discredit former editors. They had labored

under a numbing handicap I did not—that of answering to fifteen different voices, those of the First Presidency and Quorum of the Twelve. Any of these could and did call to express displeasure about what was in or not in the news or editorial columns of the newspaper. You think twice about afflicting the comfortable, even if deserved, when the potential afflictee may be the cousin or friend of one of those who felt authorized and didn't hesitate to make such a call.

My great advantage, a main reason we could accomplish what we did in the first five years of my editorship, was that by the time of my appointment, Gordon B. Hinckley of the Council of the Twelve was chairman of the board and president of the Deseret News.

This remarkable man, with long experience in media affairs, was knowledgeable and wise, with inspired instincts about the right course to take. Moreover, he was courageous. Though a junior member of the Quorum of the Twelve, eighth in line in a body where seniority weighs heavily, he announced to his colleagues that there would be no more criticism or requests from them directly to the paper's management or staff. Any such communication was to go through him. That ended the problem of multiple direction, with one exception; I continued to receive memos of instruction from senior apostle Ezra Taft Benson.

"What should I do about them?" I asked Hinckley one day. "Should I answer them, go talk to him, or what?" Though he was five chairs junior to Benson in the Quorum, his answer was unhesitating: "You have a round file, don't you? Put them there."

I did, which was wonderfully liberating. My lack of responsiveness may have had something to do with the fact that my management of the paper did not long survive Benson's becoming president of the Church. Even if so, it was worth it; by then I was nearing retirement anyway.

An even greater factor in our success was Hinckley's policy of a private lunch with me every week he was in town and not otherwise committed. Occasionally, I would bring along a staff member to discuss a specific issue in which he was involved, but usually our meetings were one-on-one. Nothing could build confidence and courage more effectively than meeting and consulting regularly with and having the full support of the man who had guided the Church media relations for years and understood the sensitivities as did few if any others.

Our meetings were informal, our discussions wide-ranging. On one occasion he said, "Bill, you're bishop of the Federal Heights Ward. My son Richard is getting interested in a girl in that ward, Jane Freed. What can you tell me about her?"

Jane was the daughter of Dave Freed, an icon of Utah tennis and my dear and highly respected friend. He was not a Mormon, which may have prompted Hinckley's question, but he lived the Church's standards and shortly before his death was baptized. Jane was all a man could hope for in a daughter-in-law, so my answer was blunt: "Gordon, if your son is good enough for Jane Freed, he must be quite a man." If that offended him, he didn't show it, and some months after they were married said to me, "About Jane Freed. You were absolutely right."

At another of our lunch meetings, I observed that as written the temple covenant of chastity did not cover homosexual relations. Not long after, it was changed to be all-inclusive.

With confidence born of such support, I made some bold moves to change the image of the *Deseret News*. The boldest was a plunge into investigative reporting. We organized what we called the Pinpoint Team under direction of City Editor Lou Bate, with a charge to ferret out and bring to light improprieties, mostly in governmental and corporate affairs, that the public needed to know about. Its members differed widely in experience and temperament.

Bob Mullens was a veteran and hardened newsman who, years earlier, had won the paper's only Pulitzer Prize for his tireless reporting of a murder at Dead Horse Point and the subsequent manhunt in southeast Utah's rugged canyon country.

Joe Costanzo, an Italian Catholic quite at home on our Mormon newspaper, was a bulldog in getting at the facts, with a soft-spoken, affable demeanor that lulled many a subject into revealing more than he intended.

Dale Van Atta was a youngster fresh out of BYU journalism school. Brash, impetuous, unpolished as a writer, he was what we called a "project." But he was a self-starter and tireless, willing to work uncounted hours when he got the scent of a promising exposé. His months of digging into the murky affairs of the murderous LeBaron polygamous clan resulted in stories that won the top awards for both Investigative Reporting and General Excellence from the Sigma Delta Chi professional journalism fraternity. The awards were particularly gratifying to me, since I had fought hard for publication of the polygamy series, against some in the Church power structure who wanted to avoid that subject. The series and other such work caught the attention of Jack Anderson, whose Pulitzer-winning column out of Washington ran in more than 600 papers. He hired Van Atta away to become his assistant, with the understanding he would inherit the column when Anderson retired. For reasons I never learned, that didn't happen.

In another move to shed the paper's image of complacency, I installed Rod Decker as an at-large columnist protector of the public interest. He had been a neighborhood kid I taught in a seventh grade LDS seminary class. Watching him grow, I had recognized an intellect and independence of thought that I felt would make him an asset in our effort. He certainly was. Typical of many of his columns that rattled the Establishment was one that criticized the grand jury system and sent Utah State Bar Association president James Lee into a rage. "I was damned mad," a *Utah Holiday* magazine article quoted Lee as saying. "But looking back, I'm not so certain I don't agree with what they were trying to say." Sadly, though, one of Decker's columns brought the beginning of the end of our aggressive investigative reporting.

A third move was to hire Calvin Grondahl as our editorial cartoonist. I had admired the creativity and sharp, somewhat irreverent wit he had demonstrated as cartoonist for the *BYU Universe*. I knew that his work would give me headaches but felt that what he added would be worth that. The headaches did come. Grondahl constantly pushed the envelope, which I tolerated as far as—and sometimes beyond—what prudence allowed. I fielded plenty of complaints, but the readers loved him.

A fourth move I knew would raise controversy was to install Joe Bauman as the first environmental specialist in the Intermountain area. It didn't take him long to plunge into such issues as Utah Power & Light plans to build a nuclear power plant, air quality amendments in the legislature, and the radioactive tailings at the old Vitro plant.

To all of these diggers into the suspicious or improper, I emphasized that to be published an investigative story had to meet the following criteria: Is it accurate? Is it provable or at least substantiated by a second reliable source? Is it fair and balanced? And, perhaps most problematical, is publishing it necessary for the public good? We sometimes stumbled in meeting that standard, but not for lack of trying.

Finally, as a sort of counterbalance, I commissioned University of Utah journalism professor Milton Hollstein as an ombudsman for our readers and a critic of our performance. He was given free rein and a column in our paper as needed to air readers' complaints and to point out imbalance, inaccuracy, bad taste, or any other evidence of poor journalism he discovered in our news or editorial coverage. His outside, independent surveillance, the first, I believe, to be established in Utah journalism, did much to help us meet our standards.

This kind of activist journalism caused understandable heartburn among those caught in the crosshairs of the Pinpoint Team, and they frequently lashed back. Most of the complainants were in responsible positions in corporations or various levels of government. In a society so dominated by Mormons, it was inevitable that many would be of that faith. In the countless hours I spent listening to their grievances, I don't remember any who didn't protest they were innocent—or that even if they weren't they shouldn't be betrayed by their own newspaper. Many of the complaints came directly to me and could be promptly handled. Others came to Hinckley and were the subject of our weekly lunchtime talks. He was stern when appropriate but always wise in his counsel of how I should handle the complaint, and never failing in his support.

Among the many peace-making talks he counseled, I especially remember two—one with Presiding Bishop Victor L. Brown and one with general authority Seventy Marion D. Hanks. Neither was personally involved in the behavior under scrutiny, but both had a financial interest in the company involved. Both talks were frank and vigorous. Both ended with a handshake of brotherhood and mutual respect—Brown (first owner and occupant of the condominium where we now live) to remain among my strongest supporters on the Deseret News board of directors, and Hanks (whom I first met in 1948 when our respective teams tangled in the All-Church Basketball Tournament; he had the sharpest elbows of anyone I ever faced on the court) to remain a treasured friend.

Though our investigative reporting cost me many uncomfortable hours, it did something far more important. It instilled in our entire staff an excitement and pride in being journalists, especially in being part of a newspaper that was making a difference. As city editor Lou Bate was quoted in an independent magazine's story: "There's a sense of excitement at the paper that's almost palpable. We've been jerked out of our rut. Our batteries are recharged."

Equally important, it won the respect of the community. Three evidences of that respect:

In a *Utah Holiday* magazine article titled, "Tired Blood in the A.M.: Clout in the Afternoon" (May 1978) Paul Swenson and Al Church wrote: "The all-encompassing stereotype that still hangs over the *Deseret News* like a cloud for many non-Mormon readers is the assumption that the paper is a house organ for the LDS Church.... Tell that to angry correspondents who have been filling *Deseret News* letters columns in recent months with pained cries of outrage and betrayal, asking how the church-owned paper could 'attack' an institution such as the Provo Canyon School, an independent facility for problem boys, with active Mormons in its administration. In a series of stories before Christmas, Bob Mullins and Joe Costanzo documented cases of physical and mental abuse at the school and unlicensed use of drugs resulting from an institutional philosophy of strict disciplinary control. 'It is really quite shocking,' wrote one respondent, 'that you would allow this kind of investigative report to be printed in your newspaper.'" The *Utah Holiday* article included a partial list of eleven other investigative stories or series of stories published in 1977 alone.

Allen Moll, both a practicing attorney and broadcast journalist, interviewed for a story in *MountainWest* magazine (August 1978), summed up his feelings: "I never would have thought that it would be the *Deseret News* that we would look to as the best local paper, much less a paper that is doing the kind of digging that it is doing—it's incredible.... I think it's great. And it's an enormous credit to the church, it seems to me, because, after all, it's their paper and there is no need on their part to have anything other than an ordinary run-of-the-mill newspaper if that's what they wanted it to be."

Perhaps the most surprising comment came from the University of Utah campus, where for years disdain for the *Deseret News* had been heavy. (In 1973, shortly after he was appointed president of the University, I lunched with David P. Gardner to discuss what we could do to dispel that disdain. His suggestions were helpful, and we became friends.) An article by

Andrew Welch in the May 31, 1977, *Daily Utah Chronicle* was critical, as college students usually are, of all the media except the *Deseret News*, which, it said, "has taken the lead in news reporting.... the *News'* health is in direct contradiction to national trends of dying afternoon newspapers and healthy morning papers. Much of the credit has to go to Smart, who has allowed his editors to try new methods of reporting and the freedom to examine tough issues."

The Ethics Challenge

Ever since its founding in 1922, the American Society of Newspaper Editors has promulgated a code of ethics and standards for the profession. The code has evolved over the years but has always emphasized truth and accuracy, fairness, integrity, independence from conflicts of interest, impartiality, and respect for the rights of persons in the news. In my day as editor, there was emphasis on readers' sensitivity; today there is only a statement about observing "common standards of decency." Shortly after becoming editor, I was appointed regional chair of the American Society of Newspaper Editors committee on ethics and standards. The years 1976 and 1977 brought an unusual cluster of cases testing how well we ourselves were meeting those guidelines.

One was that of Gary Gilmore. His 1976 execution-style murder of Orem service station attendant Max Jensen one night and of Provo motel manager Bennie Bushnell the next put him on death row. Several aspects of the case gave him national notoriety and made him the subject of Norman Mailer's Pulitzer Prize-winning book *Executioner's Song*. One, unfortunately for him, was that his conviction came just after a Supreme Court decision ended a decade-long moratorium on the death penalty; if carried out, his would be the first legal execution anywhere in the country in that time. Another was that he rejected a Parole Board hearing to spare his life and demanded early execution. "It's my life and my death, and I accept it," he declared, in effect telling the board to butt out. A third was that his death date was twice postponed by his two suicide attempts.

The second of these gave us a painful ethics decision. Our talented young editorial cartoonist Calvin Grondahl produced a cartoon showing Gilmore lying in a coma, five uniformed officers standing at the foot of his hospital bed with rifles leveled, and a nurse saying, "Wake up, Mr. Gilmore. It's time for your shot!" Should we publish it? Reluctantly, I ruled that, though brilliant, it was too sick for the sensitivities of our readers.

We faced an even more difficult ethical dilemma in the Gilmore case. During his trial, one of our young reporters, Tamara Smith, befriended Gilmore's 19-year-old girlfriend, Nicole Baker. From her she obtained, exclusively, hundreds of pages of letters he wrote her from prison describing his feelings about life and death and the reasons he committed murder, inviting Nicole to commit suicide to be with him, with many ardent protestations of his love for her. Also included were a dozen or more drawings of Nicole and other subjects, showing considerable artistic talent. It was sensational material. Word got out, and I was besieged by offers of big money from the Eastern tabloid press to obtain it. We refused all these, but faced a hard decision. What could and should we print without lapsing into sensationalism, glamorizing the killer, and raising public sympathy for him? Our answer was to publish only what was germane to the case, none of the love stuff, and to balance that with background on the victims and their families.

Gilmore was executed Jan. 17, 1977, six months after the murders, unlike killers who today languish twenty years or more on death row.

Another test of our sense of journalistic ethics came in 1976 after a will supposedly hand-written by Howard Hughes, America's richest man and most famous recluse, who had died weeks earlier, mysteriously appeared at headquarters of the LDS Church. Among beneficiaries, it named the Church to receive a sixteenth ($156 million) of his $2.5 billion estate. Another sixteenth was to go to Melvin Dummar, an obscure Tremonton service station operator. He claimed to know nothing about the will, but recalled that years earlier he had picked up a dirty, unshaven man on Highway 95, 150 miles north of Las Vegas, had driven him to the Sands Hotel there and given him a quarter. Hughes left no other known will, and his potential heirs declared this one a forgery. The case ended up in court.

We heard rumors that Dummar had been charged with but not convicted of passing an altered payroll check in Nevada some years earlier. We flew a reporter to Ely to bring back the full court record, and we studied it carefully. We knew that no trial judge would admit it as evidence and that publishing it would be prejudicial, so we didn't. Two days later, a Las Vegas paper did publish, the wire services picked it up, and it appeared in the *Salt Lake Tribune* and on local television. We felt this was irresponsible journalism, and said so in a front-page statement.

Another local test involved Utah congressman Allen Howe. In the middle of his reelection campaign, he was caught in a police sting for soliciting prostitution. A recording made of the conversation including the sex act he desired, and the price was included in the arrest report. Should we print it? A few years earlier, I had helped draft Utah press, bench, and bar voluntary guidelines on what should and should not be published to protect the right of fair trial. Publishing that conversation would be a clear violation of the guidelines, and we refrained. But television news carried it Sunday evening and the *Tribune* published it Monday morning. Rather than seen to be shielding Howe, we published it Monday afternoon. It was a bad decision by all of us. Howe continued his campaign for reelection but was defeated.

There were other ethics decisions with which we as well as the national press wrestled about that time.

Speaking to a political rally, Vice President Nelson Rockefeller was heckled by a group of students. Apparently unable to find words to express himself adequately, he responded with an upthrust middle finger, a gesture familiar to most Americans but not ordinarily used on the lecture platform. An alert photographer caught the moment. Should we publish the picture? Many editors did, feeling it said something about the character of the vice president. We did not, out of concern for the sensibilities of our readers.

A powerful Congressman, Rep. Wayne Hays (D-Ohio), admitted an amorous relationship with his secretary, Elizabeth Ray, who claimed that her $14,000 yearly salary was solely to maintain that relationship, stating that, "I can't type. I can't file. I can't even answer the phone." The wire services obtained from *Playboy* magazine and sent to newspapers a photo of her reclining on a couch, nude from the waist up. For reasons of decency we did not publish it. Only four of 300 U.S. editors surveyed did, but the photo was widely used in the European press.

On an airplane trip with other members of the administration, Secretary of Agriculture Earl Butz told an obscene joke targeting African Americans. It leaked to the press, and the Secretary was forced to resign. The *Deseret News* and most newspapers used ellipses in place of two especially vulgar words.

During a Boston tenement fire, a young mother and her pre-school child climbed out on a fire escape. Just before a fireman could rescue them, the fire escape collapsed and they fell, the woman to her death, the child surviving. A photographer snapped a Pulitzer Prize-winning shot of the two in mid-air, the fire fighter watching from above. Today, there would be no hesitancy in publishing such a picture. In my day we had more concern about portraying victims. But the photo made such a powerful statement about the heroism of fire fighters, the horror of fire, and the tragedy of living in such conditions that we published it, as did most other newspapers.

And there were the Watergate tapes, released two years earlier after a fierce legal battle. We had no qualms about publishing relevant parts, including the "smoking gun" segment in which Nixon ordered the CIA to obstruct the FBI investigation. But what of the barracks room language heard throughout the tapes? Did our readers need to read it to understand what kind of man was in the White House? We felt they did, but out of concern for the sensibilities of our readers used ellipses to indicate omission of the worst language. Most newspapers handled it that way.

I prepared a lecture titled "You're the Editor," describing each of these eight stories as a case study, and presented it to a number of diverse audiences, including an ethics seminar of Pacific Northwest newspaper editors in Portland. Listeners were invited to indicate on a prepared ballot whether or not they would publish in each case. A discussion followed about their reasons and about what the Deseret News did and why.

The results were both predictable and surprising. Overall, Pacific Northwest editors were by far most likely to publish, but were least likely to publish the Elizabeth Ray picture and the Earl Butz ethnic joke. Next most likely to publish were University of Utah faculty members and their wives. Least likely were government officials and criminal justice officials, though, surprisingly, justice officials were most likely to publish the Gilmore letters, and government officials most likely to publish the Rockefeller gesture. University of Utah journalism seniors were generally much more likely to publish than the same group at Brigham Young University, except for the death fall and the Dummar arrest record. Rotarians were generally the group least likely to publish, except were more likely to publish the Elizabeth Ray picture, possibly influenced by the request of one Rotarian that to make up his mind he had to see it again.

Using a full page and a half, we printed these case studies, inviting *Deseret News* readers to make their own judgments then compare their responses to those of the lectured groups. On the same pages we wrote of a lightly-clad Salt Lake City teenaged cross-country skier who became lost in a nearby canyon. Searchers following his tracks found his frozen body. One of them snapped a picture showing the body half covered with snow, the face not visible, his faithful dog curled up beside him. Because it illustrated the importance of proper clothing and preparation in the outdoors, was such a moving statement about the relationship of a boy and his dog, and was simply a superb photo, we published it. Some readers criticized the decision. Others told us it should win an award for outstanding photojournalism.

Who was right? Readers must decide for themselves, I wrote. There are no rules. But the incident does dramatize the decision the editor must make day after day about what goes into the newspaper and what stays out. A newspaper lives or dies by those decisions. The editor walks a fine line. He must keep his paper interesting, lively, entertaining, aggressive, newsy; otherwise it can die of dullness. But he must also keep it responsible and truthful, ethical, fair, sensitive to the feelings of its readers; otherwise, it can die of distrust."

So how are we doing with the *Deseret News*? I asked. Not as well as we would like, but better than newspapers generally, as evidenced by a national Gallup study of readers' attitudes and a poll of our readers asking the identical questions. The result:

Do newspapers give undue emphasis to the negative?

Nationally, 76% yes; *Deseret News* 47%

Do newspapers tend to convict the innocent?

National 77% yes; *Deseret News* 31%

Do newspapers not get the facts straight?

National 67% yes; *Deseret News* 29%

Do newspapers tend to slant the news, either to the liberal or conservative side?

National 80% yes; *Deseret News* 55%

This project involving our readers in and helping them understand hard decisions every editor faces received national attention in our profession. Our entire package was published on four full pages of the American Society of Newspaper Editors bi-monthly journal (May/June 1978).

Frustrations

It would be unrealistic, of course, to expect that all this could be accomplished without setbacks and frustration. We had them, especially in the early years of my editorship. In 1973, the year of Watergate leading to President Nixon's resignation, for example, I arrived at the office and found no editorial had been written about his defiance of the Supreme Court's order to turn over the Watergate tapes. I wrote what I felt—and still feel—was a balanced, temperate and badly needed editorial in defense of the Constitution. Gordon Hinckley reviewed it with Church president Harold B. Lee and reported that President Lee ordered it killed and replaced with a positive editorial expressing faith in America and confidence it would survive this crisis. Two days later, another signal came from President Lee: There was to be no editorial criticism of President Nixon. As a result, the *Deseret News* was probably the last newspaper in America to print a negative word about Nixon.

"I have faith in the inspired leadership of President Lee," I wrote in my journal, "but find it difficult at times to accept his reluctance to let us comment cogently on current matters." This was written about a man who was my neighbor, who had ordained me his bishop, who had given me a priesthood blessing before my open-heart surgery, whose daughter Helen and her husband Brent Goates were our dearest friends, in whose home our study group of friends had frequently met.

Ironically, two pages later in my journal is recorded my proposal to the Sunday School general presidency, as a member of the general board executive committee, that we sponsor in the Tabernacle on March 28, 1974, a celebration of President Lee's 75th birthday. The proposal was accepted, but it never happened. Sadly and shockingly, after only eighteen months in the office President Lee died, December 26, 1973, age 74.

Other instances of censorship gave me heartburn that year. We had to pull back and destroy 87,000 copies of the June 2, 1973, *Church News* (400 copies survived, having been mailed to Hawaii) because of an article by distinguished University of Utah geologist and my long-time friend, Dr. William Lee Stokes, attempting to harmonize science and religion on the story of creation. I thought it was beautifully, reverently, and convincingly done, but, knowing of his long-time dispute with apostle Joseph Fielding Smith on the subject, I probably should have been more circumspect. I certainly should have insisted on a less provocative title than "Which? Genesis or Geology?"

That same month, the First Presidency ordered us to refuse advertising for the movie "Jesus Christ Superstar," which was being reviewed around the country as a deeply reverential movie, was rated "G," and was described as one of the greatest movies of all time. I argued that it was not only a great movie, but that by refusing to advertise it, in violation of our own policy of advertising "G" and what were then called "GP" movies, we would be subjected to a great deal of public criticism and ridicule. I set up a private screening for the First Presidency to see the film for themselves, but Hinckley felt they were immovable, so no invitation was issued. As far as I know, none of them ever saw it. The ban stood and the ridicule followed. But we survived.

There were other such problems, but considering my determination to publish an influential, reliable, and courageous newspaper, though one owned by a conservative church with broader and different priorities, they were remarkably few. They became fewer as years went on. One probable reason was that strong-minded and politically attuned President Lee was succeeded by the less-assertive and more tolerant Spencer W. Kimball. That, I think, gave Hinckley more influence in his efforts to support and defend what we were doing. Or it may have been simply my own growing sensitivity to how far we could and could not push the envelope.

Unrealized Dreams

Early in my time as editor, I had two large dreams. One was to build a mini-chain of newspapers serving Mormon Country, from the Rexburg-Idaho Falls area on the north to St. George on the south. With each of them we would distribute the *Church News* and provide selected *Deseret News* editorials and features to supplement their local news coverage. The other dream was to publish weekly a *Christian Science Monitor*-type tabloid covering and discussing secular affairs and features from a Mormon point of view. With the *Church News*, this would be distributed with papers in the Deseret News chain as well as by mail to subscribers throughout the Church. The chief disappointment of my career is that neither dream became reality.

My efforts to build a newspaper group started years before I became editor. In 1963, having been named by editor O. Preston Robinson as his administrative assistant (while still serving as editor of the editorial page), I was authorized by him to meet with stake presidents in the upper Snake River area to explore possibilities of obtaining or building a newspaper there. On November 23, 1963, a very bad day as it turned out, I met for breakfast with the area's seven stake presidents. To avoid starting rumors from being seen together in public, we met in the private dining room of the LDS Hospital in Idaho Falls. Before we accomplished anything, the meeting broke up when someone burst in with the news that President Kennedy had been assassinated in Dallas.

Ten years later, I was in a position to try again. Another meeting with stake presidents produced a suggestion to explore acquiring a controlling interest in the *Rexburg Standard Journal*. A series of meetings with John A. Porter, the owner, and his two sons who ran the paper brought an agreement under which they would continue to manage the newspaper under our majority ownership. While the price was being negotiated, the oldest son had a change of heart, fearing that as a smoking, lapsed Mormon he would be squeezed out of management. So that effort failed, and subsequent exploratory talks about acquiring the *Idaho Falls Post Register* got nowhere.

We came closer to success in St. George, then in the first phase of its metamorphosis from a sleepy desert town to the vacation/retirement metropolis it has become. It was obvious what was coming, and I resolved to make a newspaper there the southern anchor of our newspaper group. We focused on the *Washington County News*, a weekly paper that had served the area since 1908 but was now threatened by competition from a new weekly, the *Southern Utah Press*, established by a Davis County publisher, Gail Stahle. I felt confident that with the *Church News* and other strengths the *Deseret News* would provide, the *Washington County News* would not only survive, but, with the certain population growth of the area, would become a successful daily paper.

James E. Faust, chair of the board's executive committee, and I flew to St. George and obtained from its owner, Frank Mountford, an option to buy the *Washington County News* for

$82,500. For various reasons, chiefly the opposition of *Tribune* publisher Jack Gallivan, our partner in the NAC, and his warnings about possible anti-trust problems—which our legal advisers discounted—our board of directors vacillated. Hinckley, chair of the board, wanted to finalize the purchase. Monson, vice chairman, demurred, saying, "I don't want to be the first to violate the spirit of the [Joint Operating Agreement] contract."

Weeks went by with much discussion but no decision. As Faust put it, the board was having "a stupor of thought." Two days before the option would expire, I phoned Ralph Atkin, the attorney representing us in St. George, instructing him to negotiate an extension of the option. He did, reporting he obtained a verbal two-week extension. Near the end of that period, the board finally reached a decision to go ahead with the purchase. I wired to Atkin checks of $5,000, $10,000, and $25,000, with instructions to use whatever was necessary to get Mountford's signature on a sales contract.

Three days later, Atkin called to report that Mountford had decided not to sell. Protests that he was obligated were fruitless; he replied that he had signed no extension. My response that he was morally if not legally bound left him unmoved. There was no point in discussing legal action, since I knew our owner, the LDS Church, had no stomach for that. My dream of a Mormon Country newspaper network died that day, March 5, 1973.

The outcome was predictable. Mountford's paper struggled to stay alive, and finally folded in 1988. Stahle's paper prospered, eventually becoming a daily. In 1984, we learned that Stahle was looking for a buyer. Monson, now our board chairman and having had a change of heart, said we should explore buying it. The asking price of six million dollars was judged too high, and it was sold to the Thompson Newspaper Group, presumably at or about that price. In 2000, probably worth twice that much, it was acquired by Gannett, the nation's largest newspaper group, joining 96 other dailies and *USA Today*. I never visit St. George today and heft the *Spectrum*'s fat advertising sections without a pang of regret about what might have been.

My companion dream was to publish a weekly national newspaper comparable to the *Christian Science Monitor*. I proposed as a first step that we publish a weekly section of the *Deseret News* with news and features chosen for Mormon readers and distribute it with the *Church News* throughout the

Church. I met with stake presidents and other prominent Mormons in Boston, New York, Washington D.C., and Los Angeles to get their evaluations and suggestions, and was encouraged by the response. Gallivan discouraged that also, and our board, entirely too willing, I felt, to allow him to influence our decisions, failed to approve it.

Thinking even farther outside the box, I conceived and presented to the board a plan to involve Brigham Young University, the missionary system, the Church Public Affairs Department, and the Church media (the magazines, KSL, and the *Deseret News*) in a cooperative program that would strengthen them all and make possible eventual production of the national newspaper. The concept got a favorable response from some, but as far as I know was never discussed at the highest decision-making level.

Though we never managed to create a national edition, the concept survives. Today's vastly restructured and refocused *Deseret News*, enabled by the ease of cyber-circulation, offers online a modest weekly national edition that it claims, at this writing, helps make it one of the nation's fast-growing newspapers.

A Year of Changes

By 1977, five years after my promise on that cold December day to build a courageous, professional, well-written newspaper, the results of our efforts were gratifying. While circulation of afternoon newspapers was declining nationwide, ours was growing. Independent publications were calling us "the best local paper," one that had "taken the lead in news reporting." The fine work of our staff won for me the Distinguished Service to Journalism award from Brigham Young University in 1977 and from the University of Utah in 1978.

Perhaps another indication of the stature the *Deseret News* had achieved was an invitation from the White House. Six weeks after his inauguration in January 1977, President Carter invited a dozen editors, including me, to the first of what he planned to be a series of meetings with the nation's editors. For most of a day, we met with senior members of his staff, culminating in an hour of free-flowing give-and-take with the president.

He came across as relaxed, self-confident, comfortable in his own skin, and also candid to the point of bluntness. Much of our discussion involved his opposition to nineteen reclamation projects, including the Central Utah Project, stricken from his budget that week because, he said, "I consider [them] to be a total waste of the taxpayers' dollars." When I challenged the wisdom of axing a project like the CUP on which millions of dollars had already been spent, he minced no words: "Several of these projects—I am not going to single them out—would be better not built if they didn't cost anything, if they were free."

I liked that kind of straight talk. I liked the fact that after the election his staff compiled in 110 pages all the campaign promises he had made, which he sent to the nation's editors to help them hold him accountable. And I liked that instead of the wining and dining you'd expect from a president trying to woo the press, he served us sandwiches, beer, and soft drinks. A man like that, I concluded, is likely to be one of our better presidents or one of our worst.

Sadly, candidness, transparency, and a resolve to do things your own way don't always work in Washington. Congress rejected his reclamation policies, and from there his administration spiraled downward to the seizure of the American embassy in Iran, the 444 days the hostages were held there, the botched rescue attempt that killed eight American servicemen, and to his final humiliation of seeing the hostages released minutes after his successor, Ronald Reagan, was sworn into office. But though he failed as president, this good man through his tireless worldwide humanitarian and peace efforts has proven to be our finest past president.

If 1977 wasn't a great year for President Carter, it wasn't my best either. Three events that year portended that the high-water mark the *Deseret News* had reached wouldn't last. The first was the loss of Gordon B. Hinckley as the company's president. Legal concerns about media concentration in the Salt Lake market led to a decision that he should no longer preside over both the Deseret News and Bonneville Communications with its KSL properties. So he remained at Bonneville and was replaced at the paper by its vice president, Thomas S. Monson. I had and have the highest regard for Monson, both as a much-loved church leader (he later became president of the LDS Church) and in our professional relations. He was an effective and highly regarded executive who treated me fairly and generously. But there would no longer be anything like the weekly luncheons with Hinckley that had provided such wise counsel and support and given me such confidence.

The second event was our printing on September 13 of a column by Rod Decker charging that the Public Service Commission's approval of the creation by Mountain Fuel Supply (the predecessor of Questar) of a dummy corporation to control its oil production was a consumer rip-off. Aware that N. Eldon Tanner of the First Presidency and Apostle Neal Maxwell, a close friend, were directors of MFS, I could and probably should have been more cautious. But, flushed with the success of our investigative efforts, in a burst of over-confidence I approved publication, gambling that Tanner and Maxwell, for both of whom I had and still have the greatest love and respect, would share my idealistic feeling that our role as public watchdog outweighed personal considerations.

I was wrong. President Tanner was incensed, as was made abundantly clear as I met the next day with Monson and Faust. That was followed by a meeting with them, Tanner, Maxwell, MFS attorney and former governor Calvin Rampton, and MFS vice president John Crawford. Tanner felt his integrity had been impugned and demanded a retraction, but settled for an editorial explaining what the Public Service Committee was trying to do and putting MFS in a better light.

Six weeks later came the third event. On November 2, Monson ushered me, Kay Schwendiman, manager of the Deseret News Press, our commercial printing arm, and Russ Gallegos, our comptroller, into the office of President Tanner, where Tanner announced that Wendell J. Ashton was being named executive vice president of the Deseret News Publishing Company, and that all three of us would be under his direction. Ashton would also become Deseret News publisher, but I would remain as editor and general manager.

I have no evidence that these three events were related. But it seemed strange that what amounted to my demotion came at a time when, as both Tanner and Monson declared in announcing it, the paper had never been in better shape financially, in the excellence of its staff, or in public acceptance than it had become under my direction. It seemed clear to me that I had been judged too aggressive in making the Deseret News a fearless champion of the public's right to know, and that more cautious (read church-sensitive and business-friendly) direction was needed.

Ashton was an obvious choice to give it. He had been the paper's managing editor when I joined the staff in 1948, but had left soon after to head the area's second largest advertising/public relations firm. After a successful career there, he became head of public relations for the LDS Church.

Understandably concerned about what this change would mean to the paper's future and my own, I sought explanations and counsel. In a private meeting with Monson, he explained, as my journal records, that "this move came as a result of campaigning by a number of people to appoint a publisher with whom none of us could possibly work." I took this to refer to "campaigning" by John Birch-type critics close to President Ezra Taft Benson, trying to put one of their own there. When I expressed my feeling that there would be one too many people in the management line and it might be time for me to move on, he urged me to "wait until the dust settles and see how things work out."

Gordon B. Hinckley was no longer associated with the Deseret News, but because of our long and close association, I sought his counsel. He said he could give me no information I didn't already know but confided he had spoken strongly against the move. He spoke with sadness of the way the Church had so often misused people by bringing them along to positions of responsibility and then discarding them. He said he had been thinking about this a great deal the past two weeks and had no answer for me, but, knowing the people involved, counseled that if a good opportunity came along I should accept it.

The next day, some of my staff and I had lunch with Jack Anderson, the nationally published columnist and a long-time friend. He spoke of his feeling that because of its position on blacks, women, and right-wing extremism, the LDS Church was going to experience a period of very negative media coverage. After lunch as we walked together, he said he could feel anti-Mormon sentiment on his own staff, and asked if I could suggest a strong Mormon writer to join the staff. I told him nothing of my changing circumstances, but wondered if this could be that opportunity.

With that in mind, I met the following day with Monson and told him that for my peace of mind and planning my future I needed to know all the reasons for the change other than John Birch-type pressure. Quoting from my journal: "He replied that in no discussion had he heard any negative comment of any kind about me or the work I had done at the Deseret News. He said that the only considerations were to have a man at the policy-making head of the paper who participated fully in Church policy discussions and met frequently with the First Presidency and others, that relieving me of the responsibilities of corporate, financial, building, and other business matters would make it possible for me to run the newspaper more effectively, that I was to be the editor and general manager in deed as well as name, that Wendell himself wanted it this way. I asked him bluntly, 'Is it your desire that I remain at the Deseret News or that I look for and accept other opportunities?' He replied without hesitation that he wanted me to remain, felt I should remain, and that he felt certain that proper and satisfactory relationships could be worked out in which my role as general manager as well as editor would be clearly delineated."

With that assurance, and with no real desire to move to Washington or to become an investigative columnist, I gave no further thought to joining Jack Anderson, nor did I seek any other opportunities. Some months later, Dale Van Atta, our indefatigable investigative reporter, received and accepted his offer.

Interviewing President Jimmy Carter, 1977

Kicking off the Deseret News-sponsored Mormon Trail Relay

CHAPTER EIGHT

Life with Wendell

Wendell J. Ashton was a man who deserved respect and got it. With unbounded energy and self-assurance, he had established himself as a leader in community as well as church affairs. He started early, becoming at age 35 managing editor of the *Deseret News* and national president of the Sons of Utah Pioneers. After only eighteen months as managing editor, he left journalism behind to begin a thirty-year career in advertising and public relations—twenty-four years with Gillham Advertising Agency followed by six years as director of public relations for the LDS Church. During those years he became president of the Salt Lake Chamber of Commerce, a key player in bringing the Jazz basketball team from New Orleans to Utah, president of the Utah Symphony and by far its most effective fund-raiser, and a member of the first group of LDS Regional Representatives, then just below the general authority level of LDS Church administration.

Clearly, Ashton was well qualified by experience and, as it turned out, temperament for his role of softening the hard edge of *Deseret News* reporting and editorializing, being more sensitive to LDS Church secular priorities and more friendly to the business community. As evidence of how successfully he filled that role, near the end of his Deseret News career in 1986 he was awarded the prestigious title of Giant in Our City.

But the paper paid a price. The staff's concern about coming changes was confirmed when, shortly after Ashton's arrival, at his insistence the Pinpoint investigative team was dissolved. Its members, as well as public affairs columnist Rod Decker, all of whom I had so often defended as dedicated, reliable, and effective guardians of the public good, soon left—Decker to become a highly regarded TV news reporter, Dale Van Atta to join columnist Jack Anderson's staff in Washington, Joe Costanzo to freelance. Robert Mitchell remained on staff, but in a routine reporting role. Other key staff members left in subsequent years, including LaVarr Webb, whom I had been grooming as my successor; DeAnn Evans, our superb managing editor, and Calvin Grondahl, our sometimes irritating but always entertaining cartoonist. Finding he would no longer have the freedom that I took risks to give him, he left to practice his craft for the *Ogden Standard Examiner.*

The remaining staff was still outstanding and continued to produce a well-written, tightly edited paper that consistently won awards for superior local and regional news coverage, features, and editorializing during a difficult time. And, to his great credit, Ashton filed a major and effective role in resolving a crucial issue.

Renewing the JOA Contract; Our Fight for the Future

The 1952 Joint Operating Agreement that combined *Deseret News* and *Salt Lake Tribune* production, advertising, and circulation operations in what became the Newspaper Agency Corporation (now Media One), leaving each paper with its own separate and independent newsroom, was for a period of thirty years. Operating under it during those three decades was a mixed bag for the Deseret News. The JOA achieved its purpose, providing both papers profitability and stability after the ruinous circulation battles that had led to its formation. But Tribune publisher Jack Gallivan was NAC president, his senior staff were almost exclusively his people, and it was frustrating to our staff that policies seemed always to be set and disagreements settled in ways favorable to the Tribune. Worse, we operated all those years without a Sunday paper; our subscribers received the Sunday *Tribune* instead. That we produced a paper of stature and public acceptance despite this handicap is a tribute to a professional and dedicated staff.

1982 was the year for renewal of the Joint Operating Agreement. Ordinarily, renewal of an agreement that has achieved its primary purpose can be done smoothly and quickly. But ours was a special case. I urged, Ashton agreed, and our board and owners concurred that there must be no renewal without three major changes: publication of the *Deseret News* on Saturday mornings, restoration of a Sunday *Deseret News*, and an agreement that if its share of the combined circulation fell below 35 percent for three consecutive years the *Deseret News* would have the option of becoming a morning paper. Predictably and understandably, Jack Gallivan was adamantly opposed to all three.

Negotiations dragged on for months. They were vigorous and adversarial, but civil. Gallivan was strong, determined, and a tough opponent, but also a gentleman whom we respected. As an LDS apostle, Monson was in no position to be contentious and was by nature a peacemaker. As a participant in the negotiations but no longer an NAC board member, I had to be careful not to argue too forcefully. That was left to Wendell Ashton, who filled the role admirably.

Gallivan argued that printing a Saturday morning *Deseret News* and two Sunday papers instead of one would increase operating costs, violating the JOA principle of maximizing profitability. Moreover, he argued, it took both lines of NAC presses to print the Sunday *Tribune*; printing two Sunday morning papers simultaneously would require a great increase in press capacity and there was no room to install it. Our response was that any editorial cost increase would be ours to bear. In our industry the Sunday paper was considered to be at least a third of a newspaper's strength, in influence as well as revenue. The modest increased costs would be a small price to pay for that. As for the press problem, we pointed out that by pre-printing feature sections, a press line would be available for each paper to print its time-sensitive news, sports, and editorial sections. That procedure has been followed successfully ever since.

The option of the *Deseret News* becoming a morning paper sometime in the future gave Gallivan even more painful heartburn. It would be insane, he argued. No subscriber wants to have two newspapers covering the same area delivered to his doorstep at the same time. The loss of circulation—and of profitability—would be enormous. Our response would make no sense to any hard-headed businessman: The LDS Church does not publish a newspaper to make money. It publishes a newspaper for the same reason it insists on having a Saturday morning and a Sunday paper—to maintain Church influence and uphold Church standards in this state, its home. It is clear to any thoughtful observer that in this TV-dominated society, afternoon newspapers are fading and will eventually disappear. We will sign no renewal contract that will subject us to that outcome.

From a practical standpoint, Gallivan's position clearly made more sense. But we had a stronger one. Without those three provisions, we repeatedly stated, there will be no renewal. The Joint Operating Agreement will end, and we will go our own independent way—as a morning newspaper. That would be a drastic and risky move. Gallivan had no way of knowing whether we would actually make it, but he had to know that with the stature and public acceptance we had achieved, even without a Sunday paper, and with the deep pockets of our owners, it was a real possibility. I can only imagine the pain with which he finally signed the renewal of the Joint Operating Agreement as amended with those three provisions.

The renewal was signed on June 3, 1982. After seven months of planning by and reorganization of an enthusiastically motivated staff, on January 15, 1983, the first ever Saturday morning *Deseret News* rolled off the presses. Amidst even more excitement, the next day the first Sunday *Deseret News* in thirty years followed, complete with a Sunday Magazine and Travel, Arts and Culture, Entertainment, and Business sections.

In the following days, our worries about public acceptance vanished with reports that only 287 people had insisted on taking only the six-day *Deseret News*, that only 37 had asked to continue taking the Sunday *Tribune*, and that an extra 5,000 run of our Sunday paper had sold out. It didn't hurt that Dan Valentine, long-standing *Tribune* columnist, called that first Sunday edition the best newspaper ever published in Utah.

Switching the *Deseret News* to morning publication was far more difficult. It was achieved ten years later, but only after a long and publicly rancorous battle and because of multiple Tribune ownership changes. By the late 1990s, most afternoon newspapers had vanished, and the remaining few were struggling. *Deseret News* circulation had slipped below 35 percent of the combined circulation for three consecutive years. Under the terms we had insisted on in the contract renewal, that entitled the *News* to become a morning paper, and it announced its intention to do so. The Kearns family, who had owned the *Tribune* since 1902, were vehemently opposed.

By that time the players on both sides had changed. I had retired in 1988. Wendell Ashton was gone as well, having been sent off in 1985 to preside over the England London Mission. In 1996 the LDS Church adopted a policy that general authorities would no longer serve on commercial boards of directors, a move I and others felt was long overdue. By then, Monson was first counselor to President Hinckley in the First Presidency. It would have been unseemly for a man in that position to be engaged in a publicly contentious battle over our morning publication. I have no knowledge that removing general authorities from boards was triggered by the need to avoid that. But the timing and President Hinckley's well-known public relations adroitness make it seem likely.

Whatever the reason, Monson was replaced as chairman of the board by L. Glenn Snarr. As a green young reporter, I had worked under him when he was a tough and firm but fair city editor. I had watched his rise to the top of the highly competitive public relations/advertising business with toughness and firmness as well as integrity. Other general authorities on the board were replaced by successful businessmen experienced and not reluctant to do battle in the marketplace. On the other side, Gallivan had retired as *Tribune* publisher in 1984 and as chair of the board in 1997. Gone were the civility and sure-footed competence that through the years had won our respect as our friend the adversary. The gloves were off, and the resultant battle was not pretty.

The Kearns interests, holding a majority of the stock, flatly refused to honor the provision in the JOA renewal allowing the *Deseret News* to switch to morning publication. That refusal probably could have been overcome by going to court. But the LDS Church's reluctance to get embroiled in court battles probably would have left the papers in a stalemate. In 1997, though, in what was generally understood to be a misguided move to minimize taxes, Gallivan merged the Tribune with Tele-Communications. An effort by the Kearns interests to regain control through the courts failed, and the Tribune was acquired by AT&T and subsequently, in 2000, was sold to Dean Singleton to join his Denver-based Media News Group. Dealing with a practical businessman proved far more feasible than with an emotionally attached and litigious family, and on June 9, 2003, finally appeared the *Deseret Morning News*. That assured the paper's future as long as print newspapers survive.

After leading the paper through nine stormy years as chairman of the board, Glen Snarr retired in 2005, age 83. As he arrived at a luncheon in his honor, leaning heavily on his cane, President Hinckley, then 95, raised his own cane and called, "en garde!" One of my choice memories is of those two great men engaging in mock combat.

Travels and Outcomes

Bringing Wendell Ashton aboard as publisher, Monson had pointed out, would relieve me of business and other administrative matters, freeing me to run the news and editorial operations more effectively. It did that, though the results were mixed. It also freed me to do considerable traveling and reporting that broadened our outlook and, I feel, increased our stature as a newspaper.

1978 was an especially productive year. What started out as a tourist-type trip to Egypt and Israel turned out to be far more. It gave me a once-in-a-millenium look into Egyptian antiquity, and then made me an on-the-spot observer of and reporter on a developing watershed in Mid-East history, the Egypt-Israel peace treaty that changed that region's balance of power.

Our presence in these countries at this critical time was providential. Dr. Aziz Atiya, a renowned Egyptologist and founder of the University of Utah Mideast Center, and his wife Lola were our neighbors and close friends. In addition to that friendship, Donna had worked with him as an editor in his creation of the seven-volume Coptic Encyclopedia. The Atiyas spent each spring in Egypt and several times urged us to join them there. In the spring of 1978 we did. From a journalistic standpoint, we could not have picked a more exciting time.

Experiencing Egypt with the Atiyas was an adventure. His stature among his countrymen was best demonstrated by the reaction of a high government official when I mentioned we were traveling with them. "Aziz Atiya?" he gasped. "He's here? Do you think I could meet with him?" That kind of reverence opened doors to government officials, educators and archaeologists, and to places tourists seldom if ever see.

On the evening of the day we visited the tomb of the boy-king Tutankhamen, we were invited to dine with a group of archaeologists and scientists who that very day had opened his sarcophagus for what we were told was probably only the second time in 3,000 years. One, apparently, was in 1922, shortly after

Howard Carter discovered and opened what has been described as the most intact Egyptian royal tomb ever found. The purpose of this second opening was to collect DNA and to study the cause of its occupant's death.

During the evening, one of the chief archaeologists, who shall remain nameless, drew me aside and confided that he had surreptitiously taken photographs of the mummy. Fearing that developing the film in Egypt would expose an act considered improper if not illegal, he asked if I would take the film back to the U.S., have it developed, and return it and the prints by registered mail. This I did, but kept a second set of prints. They showed that the head of what had clearly been a handsome young man had become separated from the body. Because I felt it would be unethical to do so, we never published the photos; they remain among my papers.

Throughout our time in Egypt and subsequently in Israel, both countries were seething in ferment over prospects of a peace treaty between them. Through Dr. Aziz's prestige as well as my press credentials, I was able to probe that ferment through interviews with no fewer than thirteen high-level government ministers and spokesmen, journalists, and businessmen, to say nothing of carriage drivers and camel boys, leading to a series of special reports for *Deseret News* readers.

On the eve of Israel Prime Minister Menachem Begin's departure for the White House and peace talks being orchestrated by President Carter, Palestinian Liberation Organization (PLO) terrorists from Lebanon struck near Tel Aviv, killing 36 Israeli civilians. It was at the time the bloodiest terrorist attack in Israel's thirty-year history. On the day of the attack, I stood at the Israel-Lebanon border at a place called the "good fence" because there the guards routinely opened the barbed wire to admit Christian refugees fleeing the persecution they were suffering in Lebanon. Two days later, Israeli tanks and troops poured across that border to seek out and destroy PLO strongholds. Planes struck targets as far north as Beirut. A shooting war seemed likely to stall peace talks. But, for once, the United Nations was able to act promptly and decisively. UN peacekeeping units were stationed throughout southern Lebanon, and Israel pulled back its troops. Begin left for Washington, but only after declaring that the terrorist attack would only strengthen Israel's opposition to a Palestinian state.

In an exclusive interview, former Prime Minister Yitzhak Rabin, often a critic of Begin's hawkishness, told me essentially the same thing. "There are a number of issues on which Israelis disagree," he said. "The Palestinian matter is not one of them. All agree we will not negotiate with the PLO. We will not accept a third state."

Do you trust Egypt's President Sadat in the coming peace negotiations? I asked Rabin.

"Do I trust him?" he responded. "No. His record shows no reason he should be trusted. But would I negotiate with him? Yes. Not because he has any love for Israel; love has no place in international relations. But because he knows, as we do, that war leads nowhere. Because peace is in his self-interest as it is in ours."

In Egypt, that point of view seemed even stronger. "I'd say that 99 percent of Egyptians would applaud a bilateral agreement," Mursi Saad el Din, Egypt's national director of Information, told me. "They've had enough of sacrificing and shedding blood for the Palestinians." Huge billboards along the jammed highway from Cairo to the Giza pyramids proclaimed "God bless you, champion of peace" under a 10-foot photo of President Anwar Sadat. "He won our war: he'll win our peace," proclaimed another. "Sadat is worthy of the Nobel Prize," declared another. Those sentiments were typical of what I heard from everyone with whom I discussed politics in Egypt.

So the talks proceeded, leading to the Camp David accords, and on September 17, 1978, Sadat and Begin signed their historic peace pact, witnessed by President Carter at the White House. Sadat did get the 1978 Nobel Peace Prize, along with Begin, but paid for it three years later at the hands of an Egyptian jihadist assassin. Peace in that part of the world remains elusive, as witnessed by terrorist attacks that these days kill not 34 innocent people, but hundreds—or, on September 11, 2001, on American soil, thousands.

A solution of the Palestinian issue, a root cause of so much of this bloodshed, is nowhere in sight. The Egypt-Israel peace pact itself seems in jeopardy. The Muslim Brotherhood, in control of the Egyptian government since the 2011 overthrow of the Mubarak dictatorship, has declared it will not recognize Israel's right to exist, and that the treaty will be put to a referendum. The Muslim Brotherhood-dominated government was displaced by the military after a popular uprising in 2013, but who knows what will follow? The West's hope for stability and peace in the Mideast today seems dim at best.

Patriotism and Priesthood

The second trip in 1978 started out as a brief vacation with Donna, but may have had momentous and far-reaching consequences. We attended the annual meeting of the American Society of Newspaper Editors in Washington, then went to Boston for a visit with our daughter Melinda and family, where her biochemist husband Steven Graves was doing research in the Harvard Medical School.

It was Patriots Day in Boston, and we did the usual tourist things—watched the hanging of two lanterns in the Old North Church, listened to a patriotic address there by the black Massachusetts senator Edward Brooke, watched the scarlet-clad British regulars marching on Lexington, witnessed the first shots heard 'round the world and the ladies of Lexington rushing out to minister to their dead, then roared with the crowd at the finish of the Boston Marathon, where Utahn Ed Eyestone barely nosed out the lean Texan Jeff Wells and where BYU's Curt Brinkman, his hands streaming blood from long-broken blisters, won the wheelchair division.

All that and more I reported in what I consider some of my finest writing, published as "A Day of Pageantry and Pride" (April 20, 1978). It won that year's George Washington medal from the Freedoms Foundation at Valley Forge.

But that day also may have led to a much more significant outcome. After the Marathon, Chase Petersen, then vice president for development at Harvard and a long-time friend, and I ran our own private mini-marathon along the Freedom Trail. As we ran, he spoke of the concerns of a Harvard law professor about the LDS Church policy on blacks and the priesthood. South America's first temple was nearing completion in Sao Paulo, Brazil, and the Church no longer required that all ancestral lines had to be traced outside the country to qualify to receive the priesthood. Now it was being given unless there was clear evidence of black blood. In a country as racially mixed as Brazil, this meant that persons of mixed blood were routinely being given the priesthood. There was no way, Petersen's lawyer friend argued, the Church could legally defend on religious grounds its policy of no priesthood for blacks in America when it was so clearly being given them elsewhere.

Could I help get this message to the highest levels of Church leadership? Petersen asked. I replied that if he would put it in a letter to President Kimball, I would work with the president's secretary, Arthur Haycock, to see that it came to his immediate personal attention. He did, and I did.

That conversation was on April 19, 1978. Less than two months later, on June 8, after our monthly executive committee meeting, Apostle Monson, chairman of the board, asked me to remain. When we were alone he told me we should save space in tomorrow's paper for an important announcement.

"Can you give me an idea what it's about?" I asked.

"No. It's confidential."

"Should we save space on the front page or the first page of the local section?"

"You'll know when you hear it."

Mid-morning the next day, the call came, and I did indeed know. The story appeared not only on our front page but the next morning on front pages of papers throughout the country: The LDS Church had ended its ban on priesthood for blacks. A cheer erupted when I announced the news to the staff. After instructions about preparation and placement of the story, I made my first telephone call. It was to Chase Petersen in Boston. Both of us wept with joy that this long-time embarrassment, the cause of so much hatred toward and criticism of the Church, such a hard test of the faith and loyalty of many of its members, was finally being ended.

That such a momentous policy change should have come through a man like Spencer W. Kimball was a marvel. I recalled the night of President Lee's shockingly sudden death four and a half years earlier. Normally, as a Church president neared the end we prepared a special eight-page section on his life and ministry. President Lee's death was so unexpected we had prepared nothing.

Knowing we faced a long, hard night, the staff quickly assembled. After organizing our coverage, I went to LDS Hospital to learn what I could about his death there. I was ushered into a private office where Marion G. Romney, counselor in the just-dissolved First Presidency, and Kimball, on whom as senior apostle the duties of president had been thrust the moment of

President Lee's death, were notifying general authorities around the world. I embraced President Kimball, whispered words of love and support, and wept, partly because of the death of a great, strong leader who had also been my mentor, neighbor and friend, but partly because such awesome responsibilities had fallen on a man who seemed so unready.

Kimball had been known as an earnest, humble, loving and lovable apostle, an almost lyrical speaker. But a forceful leader? A man deeply involved and schooled in the complexities of church leadership, as President Lee had been? It did not seem likely. Moreover, he seemed so physically frail. He was only a year past open-heart surgery. Four years before that, he had lost one vocal cord and part of another to cancer. He had lost his voice completely for a time, and still spoke only with difficulty.

I felt that night that his would be a caretaker presidency. I could not have been more wrong. After what had been the most dynamic, courageous Church leadership since Brigham Young, a few staff members and I met with him in preparation for a special *Church News* section on the first five years of his ministry. I told him how I had felt that night and how I felt since. His response was typical of this great, humble man. "Yes, he laughed, "how little did we know!"

Later in this relaxed, informal interview, I asked if he would care to share how the momentous priesthood revelation came about. After some hesitation, since no details had been made public, he opened up. He told how "for some time" he wrestled with the issue, praying alone in the temple for an answer; how in a temple prayer circle with the Twelve "I told the Lord if it wasn't right, if He didn't want this change to come in the Church that I would fight the world against it the rest of my life if that's what He wanted. Then I knew the time had come...this revelation and assurance came to me so clearly that there was no question about it." Our publication of that account freed general authorities who were present at that historic meeting to describe their own affirmation that the time had come.

Seeing China With UPI

In May 1974, along with fourteen other newspaper editors from around the country, I became a charter member of the newly created Advisory Board of United Press International. In that capacity, I may not have made any great contributions to

UPI, but it certainly made a contribution to me. Hardly most important but of fond memory was my attendance at a board meeting in London. UPI wangled a rare invitation for some of us to play on Wimbledon's storied tennis courts, followed by lunch with the club Secretary and a tour of the clubhouse with its portraits of champions I had worshiped since childhood. On occasion since then, after congratulating my tennis opponent on winning or offering condolences on losing, I have demonstrated my humility and startled him by confessing that I had lost my first match at Wimbledon.

Considerably more important was a nearly three-week UPI tour of China in the summer of 1978. There were seventeen of us: Rod Beaton, president, and H. L. Stevenson, editor in chief of UPI; three UPI directors; and twelve present or past advisory board members. We came by invitation of Hsinhua, the official Chinese news agency. Its editor-in-chief, soft-spoken but iron-willed Peng Ti and seven of his senior editors accompanied us throughout our 4,000-mile travels. Their presence opened doors to top government and provincial officials, to elaborate welcoming banquets, to communes, factories, schools, hospitals, farms, historic sites. At each we were given a "tea briefing" (usually it wasn't brief) by the official in charge.

All this was instructive, though we never forgot that we were being instructed by carefully programmed communists. But traveling with our Hsinhua hosts gave us opportunity to question, test our impressions on, get further information from, and argue with men who quickly became our friends. They too were programmed communists, of course, but they were also professional journalists who spoke English, with whom we could talk and argue as equals, sharing, we hoped, a sense of professional integrity.

An example of this kind of dialogue followed an unprogrammed but insisted-on visit to what was called the U.S.-Chiang Criminal Acts Exhibition Hall near Chungking. There, a pretty, young guide explained that "tens of thousands" of political prisoners were tortured and killed here by Kuomintang secret police trained by the Americans. Under questioning, she admitted that no single American had ever been here but was inflexible in insisting they were responsible. My discussion—read argument—with one of our Hsinhua hosts on the auto ride back proved equally fruitless. But later, on a three-day riverboat trip down the Yangtze, Eleanor Thomas and I corralled Peng Ti, who as editor in chief of the official Chinese news agency had enough stature to get some changes made. The discussion went like this:

"Peng Ti, it's dishonest for your tourist literature to identify that camp as a Sino-American camp and imply that Americans were equally responsible for torture there."

"We have documents proving Americans were involved."

"Your own guide said no American had ever been at the camp. Your documents may prove that Americans trained Chinese to fight our mutual enemy, the Japanese, but surely not to do what was done at that camp."

"I believe that they do."

"Look, the SATO agreement of which your documents speak was signed in 1972 and not implemented until 1973. This camp was set up in 1937. How can you call it a Sino-American camp?"

"The documents will prove we are right."

"Peng Ti, you talk about normalizing relations with America and building bridges of friendship between our two countries. Yet your tourist literature and your guides tell lies that poison the minds of your people and can only offend Americans. Why don't you use your influence to see that this dishonesty is corrected?"

"It's something we will look into."

Whether or not he did I'll never know. Fodor's tourist guide still lists the camp by that name. I can only hope the verbiage has been changed.

A far more meaningful discussion, the highlight of our trip, was a two-hour meeting with the pragmatic Deng Hsiao-ping. Twice purged by doctrinaire Maoist communists, once during the Cultural Revolution and once by the "Gang of Four," he had been restored to office only months before our visit and was now the most powerful man in the world's most populous nation. In those months he had begun the modernizing and opening of China to the West, undertaking what he called the "Second Long March" toward technology and industrialization, and introducing the beginnings of capitalist-type methods of production incentives and private ownership of plots of land.

Deng met us on the top steps of the Great Hall of the People overlooking Tienanmen Square. I had heard he was short, but not this short; the top of his head barely reached my shoulder. Yet there was strength in his handclasp, steadiness in his gaze, a commanding air of authority in the easy way he took charge. He ushered us into a heavily carpeted reception room, seated us in deep plush armchairs, lit the first of a chain of cigarettes, hawked, spit into a spittoon by his foot, uttered the standard words of welcome and friendship, and invited questions.

For nearly two hours they came. His answers reflected little warmth toward the United States, warning there will be no normalizing of U.S.-China relations until we break off relations with and get our troops out of Taiwan. Again and again he criticized U.S. indifference to Soviet aggression, including its adventurism in Africa and the presence of Soviet pilots and technicians "right under your nose" in Cuba. His response to a question about the fate of the "Gang of Four" was puzzling. Having himself been a victim of their extremism, he said they had not been tried nor would they be.

"No punishment is great enough for their crimes. They are eating their meals as usual, and will continue to do so."

The only hard news in the interview came in response to my question. Six months earlier, I had been invited to a dinner at the Chinese diplomatic mission in Washington and had learned that the chief of mission was being reassigned. Since no replacement had been named in all that time, I asked Deng, does that indicate a cooling in U.S.-China relations? His answer was brief but conclusive; "We have just nominated for U.S. approval Chai Tse-min, who has been ambassador to Thailand and a number of other countries."

On another question I got a less concise but unmistakable answer. Before leaving for China I had been requested by LDS president Spencer W. Kimball to learn all I could about the possibility of missionaries serving there. So I asked Deng: What do you think about the future of religion in China? Will Christian churches, for example, be allowed to operate freely and do missionary work here?

His answer: "You know the history of religion in China. It must be clear to you what missionaries have done in the past. They taught that God made you poor and that's how he wants you to remain. We have done away with such oppressive superstition."

Does that mean, I persisted, that you view religion as a future threat to China's society?

Curtly: "We have in China people who believe in Christianity. Also in Buddhism, Taoism, Islam—and [with emphasis] atheism." That emphasis was understandable; two generations of anti-religious propaganda had made China a largely secular nation.

Throughout our tour I asked the same question to provincial and municipal leaders and got essentially the same answer. This negative response I reported in the first of many lectures after returning home. I also reported my impression that in some ways the Chinese of that day had values much like ours: Strong family ties, a strict code of honesty and morality, and a tradition of caring for each other, including correcting each other's behavior. Every neighborhood or commune was divided into study groups who spent ten hours or so a week studying socialist doctrine and criticizing each other's thoughts and actions. To me, it sounded like home teaching on steroids.

President Kimball attended the first of such lectures, took notes, and the next day requested and received a copy of my text. A few weeks later, to a conference of Regional Representatives he repeated much of my report on the positive aspects of Chinese society. The day was coming, he said, when China would be opened to missionary work. He urged that young people learn Mandarin and prepare in other ways to serve there. I have no doubt that day will come, but to me it seemed a long way off.

The Deseret News published a small book, *China Notebook*, containing fourteen of my articles, with photographs, as printed in the paper. "This is no attempt to pose as an expert on China," I wrote in the foreword. "That land is too vast, its people too diverse, its history and its present too profoundly different from anything we know in the West to presume to say what China was or is or will become. The essays that follow are, simply, a journalist's description of what we saw and heard and felt.... Even at that, it is a spotty record. It was as though a searchlight played over that immense land, pausing only occasionally to illuminate this town or that aspect of Chinese society."

But this much became clear: we were witnessing a crucially important watershed in Chinese history. By introducing private ownership of small plots of land and private ownership of livestock on the farms and bonuses for superior work in industry, Deng had taken small but important steps toward an economy based on the capitalist philosophy of "To each according to his work." But he and others insisted to us that the ultimate goal was pure communism based on: "To each according to his need."

"When will that happen?" we asked him. "It's a long way off," he answered.

"Indeed it seems to be," I wrote, "and in the meantime China seems to be headed in the opposite direction. Reversing course and leveling everyone into real equality would take more co-operative discipline—or bloody force—than even the Chinese can manage."

Ten years later, I returned to China, this time with Donna, to report how it turned out. The changes were startling. Construction cranes seemed to be everywhere. Instead of the hordes of bicycles, steady streams of cars filled the streets, spewing their exhaust into the already-murky air. On our first visit, we had found no imported goods in the department stores. Signs urged frugality; in effect, "If you don't need it don't buy it." This time, there were plenty of imported goods and western-type signs urging people to buy, which they were certainly doing. Clearly, China was embarked on a course to become no less than the world's second largest market economy.

But we sensed another kind of change. Instead of what ten years earlier had seemed to be stolid contentment with an existence that was stable though anything but affluent, on our second trip we heard grumblings of discontent. We heard complaints about inflation, corruption and nepotism in high places, limited career opportunities, a lack of respect and compensation for intellectuals, especially educators. Trouble seemed to be brewing.

My stories about this trip appeared in the fall of 1988. In April 1989, half a million protesters in and around Tiananmen Square demanded economic reforms, political liberalization, and freedom of the press. Even for reform-minded Deng Hsiao-ping, it was too much. He ordered a military crackdown, and on July 4 the world's press carried the iconic photo of that student standing resolutely in front of a line of four Chinese tanks about to use live ammunition to clear the square. Estimates of the dead ranged from several hundred to thousands.

After two weeks in China, Donna and I went west into Tibet. Because private travel was not permitted there, we formed ourselves into a two-person tour group and obtained visas that way. We were excited to experience something of that fabled land known as the "roof of the world," from whose mountains and vast steppes pour six mighty rivers—the Yangtze and Yellow into China, the Ganges and Brahmaputra into India, the Indus into Pakistan, the Mekong through Laos and Thailand into Cambodia—bringing water to countries housing half the people on earth.

In Tibet we found profound evidence of the tenacity of ancient cultures, ancient medicine, and ancient religion. Since China's bloody conquest and takeover of Tibet in 1951 and expulsion of the Dalai Lama in 1959, it had systematically set about to modernize this ancient country. In Lhasa, the capital, we saw the "progress" made in that effort. Ugly grey cement-block buildings had replaced Tibet's graceful architecture as China sought to displace the Tibetans with its own people. Probably half the population of Lhasa was now Chinese, we were told, and that didn't include the Chinese soldiers who seemed to be everywhere.

Yet, out on the vast grasslands an hour drive from Lhasa, at 12,000-foot elevation, life went on as it had for centuries. We saw yak trains being loaded with salt and other goods for the weeks-long trek over the Himalayas for trade in India, just as had been done a thousand years or more. As from time immemorial, platters of dried yak dung covering cobblestone walls constituted the family's winter fuel supply.

China labeled Tibet's centuries-old traditional herbal and naturalist medicine as superstition, and tried to replace it with modern scientific medicine. We could not evaluate how successful that had been. But we visited a medical school in Lhasa and found there a few Tibetan doctors still practicing traditional medicine, remaining after others had fled or been killed. We marveled at what seemed to be thousands of documents containing knowledge accumulated over the centuries.

How many are there?" we asked, and were humbled by the reply: "What does it matter? There is no end to knowledge."

China's major effort has been to destroy or greatly diminish the influence of the ancient religion, Tibetan Buddhism. Red Guards destroyed some 6,000 monasteries during the Cultural Revolution in the 1960s. The Dalai Lama was exiled in 1959 after the Lhasa uprising, during which hundreds of monks were killed. Just a year before our visit, in September 1987 while the Dalai Lama was visiting the U.S., a demonstration for independence was crushed, with many monks being killed or arrested and tortured.

Despite this sad history, from what we saw we concluded that Buddhism was alive and well. Wherever we went, what people asked for was a picture of the Dalai Lama (Travel Tip: If you go, take stacks of them if you want to be warmly welcomed). Out on the steppes, in a small monastery the Red Guards had missed, our souls were stirred by the deep-throated notes of eight-foot-long brass horns calling the faithful to prayer.

But what stirred us most deeply was the sight of ancient open-bed trucks crowded with pilgrims who had stood shoulder-to-shoulder in the icy winds for who knows how many miles over rutted roads to reach the Potala Palace in Lhasa. Carrying their jars of yak butter to flicker before what was left of the 10,000 shrines the Potala once held, they prostrated themselves caterpillar-like up the hill to the palace. Idolatry? Perhaps. But I have never failed to think of the faith and dedication of those pilgrims when I have read the Mormon scripture telling us that "the Spirit giveth light to *every* man that cometh into the world; and the Spirit enlighteneth *every* man through the world, that hearkeneth to the voice of the Spirit. And *every one* that hearkeneth to the voice of the Spirit cometh unto God, even the Father." (Doctrine and Covenants 84:45-47, emphasis added).

Up Close in Castro's Cuba

Three years after the first China tour, with a similar group of officers and advisory board members of UPI, I had another look at communism up close, this time in Cuba. Our visit was in April 1981, precisely twenty years after what was up to that time probably America's most disastrous foreign policy blunder, the Bay of Pigs invasion. Forty-two years later, our invasion of Iraq on the pretext of non-existent weapons of mass destruction, and the more than a decade of war that followed, dwarfed that blunder in terms of bloodshed and treasure, but this one was bad enough.

In a scheme hatched under the Eisenhower administration but approved by the recently installed President Kennedy, a brigade of 1,500 Cuban exiles, trained, equipped and transported by the CIA, landed at 2 a.m. April 17, 1961, at the remote Bay of Pigs in the south of Cuba. They were supposed to catch the Castro forces by surprise, march quickly inland, and be welcomed by an uprising of the Cuban people. But there was no surprise, no march inland, and certainly no uprising. In three days it was over: 200 invaders dead, 1,197 taken prisoner, 103 able to get back into their boats and flee.

In a small museum in the nearby village of Giron, we examined relics of the battle. A nearby billboard boasted, "Primera gran derrota del imperialism en America Latina." "The first great defeat of imperialism in Latin America."

It was all of that, and much, much more. It brought us to the brink of nuclear war and cemented a Russia-Cuba alliance that posed a threat for the next forty years. Emboldened by our incompetence in hatching such a plan and bungling it so badly, Russia installed nuclear missiles in Cuba by the fall of the following year. The threat of nuclear war seemed perilously real until Krushchev backed down. Immediately after the Bay of Pigs fiasco, Russia began a program of subsidizing the Cuban economy $4-6 billion a year by selling it oil at deeply discounted prices and buying Cuban sugar at greatly inflated prices. In return, Cuba acted as Russia's surrogate in fomenting Marxism in African and Latin American countries. On the Isle of Pines—then called the Isle of Youth—once the site of Batista's infamous Modela Prison, we visited schools where students from Nicaragua, Ethiopia, Mozambique, Angola, Namibia, and the Congo were being trained to do that.

Our Cuban visit had two purposes. One was to probe the possibility of establishing a UPI bureau in Havana in return for UPI support of a Cuban bureau in Washington. The other was to give a few editors a look at how Cuba was faring just at the midpoint of that forty-year alliance. Regarding the first goal, the answer was blunt: There can be no thought of exchanging bureaus until the U.S. embargo is lifted and relations are normalized.

As for the second, we talked with ministers, governors and mayors, factory superintendents, hospital and school directors, and with men, women, and children in the streets, on the beaches, and in the schools. Not, however, with Fidel Castro. The press reported his meetings with various delegations, but we were told he was "too busy" to meet with us, and took that as a deliberate anti-American snub.

We heard much about the new society—free education, free medical care, free sports and entertainment, free burial, far more schools and doctors and hospitals than before the revolution, Third World-type diseases practically eliminated, 98.5 per cent literacy, and more. We saw no evidence to the contrary.

What we did see was something less than what one might expect in such an ideal society. Havana's infrastructure was crumbling. Our own hotel, built with Mafia rackets money, reflected the opulence of pre-Castro Cuba. But its plaster was falling off the walls, mirrors were cracked, the carpet was filthy and spotted with cigarette burns, plumbing was spotty, the place smelled of mildew. For the populace, our hosts admitted, housing was critically scarce, much food rationed, most goods prohibitively expensive. All this despite the Russian subsidy of eight to ten million dollars a day.

In the faces and attitudes of the people, we saw no sign of joy in living in such a beautiful place and being cared for, cradle to the grave, by the government. What we mostly saw and felt was glumness. From no bellman, elevator operator, desk clerk, or chambermaid—and from no one on the street or beaches—did we receive a smile or pleasantry. And there was something else. A thirty-year-old man on the beach with his wife talked freely, but not critically, of life under communism—until I began taking notes. Then, apprehensively, "You're not going to write about this, are you?

"Yes, probably."

"But you won't use my name?"

"Not if you don't want me to."

"But what about that picture you took?"

"If we use it, it will be in Salt Lake City, 3,000 miles away. That can't hurt you, surely."

"But," his voice lower, pleading, "The police watch. They are very strong...."

So, no picture. But the exchange made it a little easier to understand why the ninety miles of Caribbean waters between Cuba and Florida were so frequently dotted with boats filled with people seeking to escape Castro's "new society."

Collapse of the Soviet Union in 1991 ended Russia's subsidy and with it Cuba's efforts to spread communism abroad, as my final article in the Cuba series predicted would eventually happen. "Then," I wrote, "there's the hope for evolution within Cuba itself to a more benign form of socialism. The seeds are there. Throughout the economy, Castro has introduced capitalist techniques of bonuses and other incentives. As the revolution ages, it may lose its militancy. And there's hope that by wiser statesmanship, more concern for human welfare in emerging states, more intelligent export of our ideals along with our technology, we can deny communism fertile soil for planting its seeds. It's not an easy road, or a sure one. But it's the best one open to us. Traveling it is going to take patience and perhaps more humility than America has known."

Re-reading those words a third of a century later, I am impressed that though our world, its problems, and our real or potential enemies are much different, the ultimate solution may be pretty much the same.

Terror in the Skies

Another trip involved no such momentous events but did leave us with the memory of one unforgettable night. In the fall of 1983, with Donna I attended meetings of the Inter-American Press Institute in Lima, Peru. Following the meetings, we toured Cuzco and Machu Picchu and then cruised and hiked the Galapagos Islands, resulting in what I felt were fairly insightful travel articles for the *Deseret News*. But it was the trip home that we'll never forget.

At Miami, we connected to Eastern Airlines flight 836 to Denver and Salt Lake City. Following are excerpts from an article I wrote for *Guideposts* magazine:

The captain's voice was calm: "We have a little problem here. Nothing to worry about. But we'll have to return to Miami airport.

Donna and I looked at each other as the 727 tilted into a turn. So that heavy thump we had heard shortly after takeoff had meant something. But probably nothing too serious.

So we followed instructions and didn't worry—until the flight engineer hurried through the cabin with a long screwdriver and an expression that clearly said he was worried. He looked even more worried when he returned to the cockpit and came back with a pair of pliers.

"I wonder if he needs some bailing wire," someone joked.

"Or a hairpin," a woman added.

But the mood sobered when the captain announced, "Folks, it looks like we may be making an emergency landing in Miami.

But first we'll circle while we dump our extra fuel."

Emergency landing? Dump fuel? I had flown enough and seen enough to know what that meant: a crash landing. Flooding into memory came the sight of a blackened fuselage and charred bodies, the smell of jet fuel and burned flesh in a disaster I had covered as a newspaperman almost 20 years earlier. Forty-three passengers, half of those on board, had been incinerated when a 727 like the one we were on hard-landed and burned at Salt Lake City International Airport. Was it now our turn?

A tire had blown in the wheel well of our plane, knocking out the landing gear's hydraulic system. The pilot's effort to lower the landing gear had brought the nose and left wheels down; the right wheels stayed up. The flight engineer's attempt to lower the one or raise the others manually had failed.

But all that we wouldn't know until later. All we knew now was that our future was very uncertain.

The lights below disappeared as we flew out over the Atlantic and, for more than an hour, jettisoned fuel. As we sat in the darkened cabin, I wondered how the 156 persons aboard were handling the trouble that loomed…. Donna and I held hands and spoke softly of our love for each other and our gratitude for a full life….

After a long, long hour, a stewardess began crash instructions. "Tighten seat belts. Lean forward, head on knees, arms cradling a pillow over your head."…. Stewardesses picked four capable-looking men to deploy the emergency chutes and help passengers out the doors. The instructions were terse: "Jump on the chutes feet first, arms folded. When you hit the ground, run!"….

So the time had come to live or die. The captain eased the giant jet onto the runway. The wheels touched gently as a feather. The cabin erupted in cheers. We were, we thought, safe.

But we weren't. In seconds, the landing gear collapsed, and the plane was veering and bouncing on its belly. Sparks showered beneath us. I caught a flash of orange flame in the right wing—and remembered those 43 charred bodies. Fire trucks raced alongside, pouring foam on the plane as it skidded down, then off the runway. Foam soaked the passengers as they tumbled down the emergency chutes.

After finding Donna in the darkness and confusion, I paced the distance from the foam-drenched plane to a chain link fence.

Beyond it ran a freeway where hundreds of people, alerted by newscasts about the impending crash landing, had gathered to watch.

Thirty yards. It was that close. I whispered a prayer of thanks.

Afterward, in a jam-packed airport lounge, shaken and drenched passengers downed hot coffee, scrambled for telephones to call loved ones, and described what they had thought and felt: "I thought we were goners. "I never prayed so hard in my life." "I promised God I'd quit smoking if He got us down safely."

But from a young LDS missionary returning from service in Ecuador came a statement I cannot forget. It expressed all any of us really needs to know about what God expects from and hopes for us. It has changed my life.

"What I kept thinking," he said, "was that we should live our lives always ready for a crash landing."

To Timbuktu and Beyond

In 1983-84, a devastating drought gripped North Africa, bringing widespread starvation. The LDS Church asked its members to fast, pray, and contribute to a drought relief fund. Response was overwhelming, with more than six million dollars contributed, and this became the beginning of what is now acclaimed as the Church's worldwide humanitarian program.

My own involvement was more intimate and personal. In June 1985, with five other Utahns I traveled to Mali, one of the five poorest countries on earth, where even in normal times more than half of its people lived below the international poverty line of $1.25 a day. Drought had hit especially hard there, and we went to investigate the possibilities of establishing a Utah-to-Mali humanitarian effort.

Landing at Bamako, Mali's capital, we intended to fly on Mali Airline to Timbuktu. But the airline's single plane had crashed a week earlier. We did manage to charter an ancient DC-3, and, approaching a landing at Timbuktu, spotted the charred remains of Mali Airlines beside the runway.

That sight seemed somehow emblematic of the fate of this once-proud city. During Europe's dark Middle Ages, Timbuktu was the center of West Africa's commerce and a center of learning with a library second only to the famous one at

Alexandria. It lay just where the sandy wastes of the Sahara met the dry but fertile Sahel region to the south. There for centuries gold-laden donkey trains from the negroid tribes of the south met to trade for salt brought by the camel-riding Arab-Berber tribes of the desert. But the Sahara's inexorable advance had left Timbuktu a near-dead city forty miles inside the desert. The few Tuareg tribesmen we encountered, their herds lost to the drought, were sadly reduced to selling even the emblems of their manhood, ancient rifles and ceremonial swords.

Of all the memories of that trip, none is more searing than that of a Tuareg tribesman, muffled to the eyes, his camel shambling through a sandstorm to the nearly-dry well where we were being shown the results of the drought. Obviously desperate, he appealed for water for himself and his camel. Also desperate, the villagers said they could spare none. Without a word, he rode off into the storm. It was a sad but understandable violation of the hospitality code of the desert that for centuries had made possible life there.

I had hoped we could establish an aid program that could help to rehabilitate Timbuktu. Clearly, desertification had made that impossible. We traveled 200 miles east to the hilly country beyond the bend of the Niger River to assess the possibilities of an aid program among the Dogon tribes in what seemed an especially harsh environment there.

What seemed to be the entire village, young and old, most wearing carved wooden masks, turned out to greet us with a lengthy, noisy circular dance. Then, assuming from my advanced age (I was 61) that I was the leader of the group (I wasn't), their chief gifted me a chicken and a young goat. As graciously as I could manage, I thanked him, then declared that since they might not survive the trip home, I was honored on behalf of the people of the United States to gift them to the Dogon children. Instead of being offended as I feared, their leaders seemed relieved.

Despite their hospitality, our group concluded this was not the place to establish an aid program. Instead, the choice was the Ouelessebougou region some 250 miles northeast of Bamako, where a dozen villages cluster around the town of Djenne. Since 1985, the ongoing and successful Ouelessebougou Alliance has built schools, trained teachers, dug and sanitized wells, provided dental and medical treatment including more than a thousand cataract surgeries, and provided mini-business loans to foster economic growth in that little-known, impoverished region.

Need for a Change

By 1984, seven years after Wendell Ashton came aboard and increasingly intruded into editorial and news coverage decisions, the *Deseret News* clearly bore the stamp of what he conceived to be his mission—to be "friendly" to business interests (no more investigative reporting); to soft-pedal or ignore negative coverage of LDS-related activities; that while both political parties were to be treated equally, Republicans were to be treated more equally than Democrats. During the 1984 political campaign, for example, we were not to criticize or do cartoons that ridiculed Reagan. When I protested that this was a different policy than I had seen in my 35 years at the Deseret News, Ashton said he was sure this was what the Brethren wanted.

I doubted that statement at the time, and even more so when a few weeks later, while Ashton was touring Israel with his family, Monson and Faust approved publication of a Grondahl cartoon lampooning Reagan for an off-the-record joking remark about bombing Russia. A few days after that, though, Ashton was back in the office and roasted Grondahl and me for a cartoon critical of Lt. Gov. David Monson. Since Monson, a Republican, was running in Utah's Second Congressional District against Frances Farley, a Democrat, he was now apparently untouchable. Moreover, Ashton insisted that to be published, any future Grondahl cartoon had to be approved by him. That did it for Grondahl. One of our strongest assets, he shortly left to do cartoons for the smaller *Ogden Standard Examiner*. Since then, the *Deseret News* has relied on syndicated political cartoonists.

Ashton also targeted another cartoon, the incisive critique of politics and society, *Doonesbury*. When this cartoon was first offered, I had snatched it up quickly and considered it one of our best assets. However, once while I was away at a conference of editors, my secretary called to say that Ashton had ordered him to cancel *Doonesbury*. I told him to wait. When I returned, I made it clear to Ashton that if we canceled the cartoon, the Tribune would grab it; moreover, if *Doonesbury* left the paper, I would leave also. The cartoon remained—until the moment I was "kicked upstairs." At that point, the Deseret News management cancelled Doonesbury—and the *Tribune*, immediately grabbed it.

Under the new policies, key people left the paper one by one. One was LaVarr Webb, whom I had been grooming as my successor. He told me he was thinking of going to the *Tribune*. To my relief, he didn't, but did leave to join Governor Matheson's staff. Another was DeAnn Evans. When managing editor J M Heslop was called in 1980 as an LDS mission president in Chicago, we named her to replace him. On Heslop's return three years later, Ashton insisted on restoring him as managing editor. He was unmoved by my protests that this would be unfair to Evans, who had done an outstanding job. The staff rebelled, and it was only after Heslop himself said that replacing her would be improper that Ashton finally relented. But Evans, bruised by the battle and dismayed about the direction the paper was taking, left anyway, to teach journalism at University of Utah. A number of others took early retirement, including Charles Nickersen, head of the art department, whose drawings had graced our feature section for 35 years.

Ashton's changed policies led not only to loss of good people, but also to loss of public confidence and acceptance. Circulation, which had been climbing steadily the previous few years, collapsed from 76,189 in 1977, the year he arrived, to 63,561 in 1984. *Tribune* circulation increased by 5,000 during the same period. Alarmed at the loss, we commissioned Ruth Clark, a respected media critic, to study the cause and recommend solutions. She did offer some suggestions, but her basic conclusion was clear: "The *Deseret News* has a serious image problem—all centering on its perception of being a one-sided LDS-biased paper. It is regarded as opinionated, narrow-minded, manipulative, censored, and as failing to give both sides of controversial issues." What a sad contrast that was to the way the paper had been viewed only seven years before.

I appointed committees of the staff to study the report and make recommendations, culminating in a two-day retreat at Snowbird. There, in frank discussion with Ashton present, we hammered out a report to our board of directors, emphasizing that Clark's chief concern about censorship, LDS bias, manipulation, one-sided reporting and editorializing could only be corrected at the general authority level. Omitted, at Ashton's insistence, was the committee's recommendation of a new publisher with no visible LDS Church connection.

In a preliminary meeting with the executive committee I

outlined what we intended to present, emphasizing the need for the top level of Church leadership to address our image problem. I was pleased with Monson's response that this would be done and that Gordon B. Hinckley was understanding of and desirous to help in this evaluation. I have no knowledge that this was ever done.

Pressure for Ashton's removal grew, both among the staff and at least one member of the board of directors, which put me in an awkward position. Though fully sympathetic with the staff's frustrations, I was part of management and could not be disloyal to my associate. When Emma Lou Thayne, a board member and long-time friend, sought my counsel as to whether she should meet with Monson to urge Ashton's dismissal, I demurred. "I can't and won't be involved in any way in any effort to dislodge my superior," I told her. When some staff members began circulating a petition calling for his dismissal, I met with them and strongly urged that this not go forward. If there's to be a change, I said, it should be done gracefully in a way that will allow Wendell to retire with dignity. They agreed to stop.

Finally, on March 21, 1985, the shoe dropped. Ashton and I met with Monson and Faust and they informed us of Ashton's retirement. It would be done in the same graceful way O. Preston Robinson had left 21 years earlier, a call to preside over the London North Mission, where Ashton and President Hinckley had been young missionary companions. I was to remain as editor and general manager. Surprisingly, they said they had not thought of a new publisher and asked for any suggestions I might have. I mentioned Vance Caesar, a Mormon who was publisher of the Santa Monica paper, but indicated I would think further about this.

So ended eight years of a challenging relationship. My and Ashton's philosophies about what the *Deseret News* should be were fundamentally different, which led to many pointed and vigorous arguments. But our differences were never personal. I recognized that he was doing what he thought he was hired to do and what his own convictions told him to do, and respected him for it. I feel confident he had the same kind of respect for me and recognized that, despite our differences, I had never undercut him.

Meeting with Deng Hsiao-ping, and with Chinese children in 1977

On the Great Wall of China with Donna in 1987

1984 Utah State Tennis Championship finals, over-60 division, in which Bill beat Ellsworth Hales and became ranked the #1 player in the state in his age group

Interviewing Spencer W. Kimball in 1979, five years after Kimball became president of the LDS Church

CHAPTER NINE

The Final Years at the *News*

Though it probably would have made no difference, I soon regretted the deletion of our recommendation that a new publisher should have no visible LDS Church connections. William James Mortimer, chosen as the new publisher, had been employed in Church-owned business his entire adult life, much of the time also holding highly visible Church positions. After graduating from Utah State University, he worked briefly for the Deseret News, then for the Deseret News Press, then at Deseret Book as vice president and general manager. He had been a stake president; Regional Representative, a position just under the General Authority level; and secretary of the Church Scripture Publishing Committee.

In my journal on the day of his appointment I wrote: "With his business and printing background, I feel Jim will do well in representing the Deseret News with the NAC, but I have concerns about whether he will be strong and independent enough to stand up for professionalism in the paper against the Church pressures that will come." He was a thoroughly good man, open and approachable, an effective administrator who built good relationships with the staff through a policy of open communication with individuals as well as groups of staff members. Without a change of policy by our owners, however, there was little he or I could do to change the paper's negative public image.

On November 5, 1985, death came to President Spencer W. Kimball, whom I had so much loved personally and admired for his inspired and courageous leadership of the Church, including ending the ban on priesthood for black members. Following the established policy, Ezra Taft Benson, the senior apostle, became president of the Church. I had long wondered what that would mean to me and the *Deseret News*. Within seven months, I knew.

In a June 5, 1986, meeting with the executive committee, Monson frankly discussed the right-wing attacks being made against the *Deseret News*. My journal entry: "He named the names of the right-wingers, made it clear he considered them irrational but very dangerous extremists, described how he and Gordon Hinckley conferred on this problem and won President Benson's approval of the strategy of dealing with them on a slightly lower level. Henceforth, Jim Faust and Neal Maxwell will be our point people on this matter, with Elder Monson backing them up. I feel very grateful for his strong support in this area and agree with his assessment that this is the most serious threat to the *Deseret News*."

The pressure Mortimer was feeling led to our only serious disagreement. On July 21 he informed me that our officers had instructed us to slant the news so as to avoid anything negative about Republican governor Grant Bangerter or anything positive about wilderness, and that we should edit the letters to the editor in the same way. I told him I could not believe that this is what our officers wanted and insisted we have a discussion with them to clarify this. I told him no responsible newspaperman would remain under those conditions—a clear signal that I would leave if this is what we were ordered to do. The next day, he recanted.

Still, pressure mounted. On August 6, meeting with James Faust, Mortimer, and me, Monson warned of our growing exposure because of resentment of the paper not only from right-wingers but also from agriculture, mining, and anti-wilderness groups, all of whom had access to President Benson, who could insist on a change of management at any time.

Sometime before September 8, he apparently did just that. On that day, over sandwiches, Mortimer painfully informed me that it was felt that it was time for me to step down as editor and general manager. In response to my direct question, he said that, yes, this was because of pressure from the right-wingers.

I responded that I had long known this could happen and I could accept it without rancor, but felt deep sorrow for the Deseret News, knowing it would have a profound adverse effect on the staff and that it would only feed the appetites of the right-wing for more red meat. Mortimer, I felt, was going to face a cruel choice, either capitulating to the wolves as I had refused to do, or becoming himself a victim of their attacks.

Monson insisted I not be hurt financially in any way, that he had the highest regard for the job I had done, and that anything I wanted within reason I could have. If I now chose to retire, it would be with a year of full salary and a six-month early retirement bonus. Or, I could remain at full salary as senior editor for the two years until I had completed forty years at the Deseret News, then retire at age sixty-six.

For two reasons, I chose the latter. The selfish one was that I loved the paper and hated the thought of leaving. The other was that I felt it would do the least damage to the paper. It would be less dismaying to the staff and make it less likely that the media, guessing the reason for my dismissal, would make a sensational story about it. In any event, I assured Monson, the media would get no story from me other than that it was time for younger management and I welcomed the opportunity to do what I enjoyed most, traveling and writing.

Monson specified that I was to keep my office and secretary, which I declined to do. Mortimer was now the editor and should, I felt, move immediately into the editor's office. I occupied a small office instead. Richard Christensen, my secretary, had been much more than that. I had considered him an administrative assistant, a trusted confidant and friend. He had faithfully transcribed my dictated daily journal, finally totaling 1,215 legal-size single-spaced pages, and he assembled, without my knowledge, a massive scrapbook of articles, clippings, and photographs. Both of these were invaluable resources in producing this biography. Losing my relationship with him would hurt, but there was no way I could justify keeping a secretary for what I would be doing.

My duties as outlined would be minimal. I was to spend as much or as little time at the paper as I wished, and travel and write as I wished. I was to give guidance about good writing to individual staff members as requested, and give counsel to Jim Mortimer as requested. There were few requests.

The one specific task I was asked to do was to write the weekly message for the back page of the *Church News*. That became a joy. For years, this space had been filled by what could best be described as short, doctrine-heavy sermons written by Apostle Mark E. Petersen. My contributions were mini-essays, mostly based on personal experience, observation, and reflection. Deseret Book published a selection of these under the title

Messages for a Happier Life. The market for Mormon books being what it is, this slender volume brought more royalties than the total of six far more ambitious and effort-demanding books published since my retirement.

To Asia's Under-Belly

The invitation to travel and write as I saw fit resulted in my final two such trips for the Deseret News. The final one, previously discussed, was in 1988 to examine the dramatic changes in China in the ten years following the first trip there and the state of Tibet under Chinese rule. The next-to-last, in 1987, took me to a part of the world that was unsettled and dangerous then and has become even more so in the years since.

With a small group of editors sponsored by the Center for Strategic and International Studies, I traveled to India and Pakistan, two nations that had recently armed themselves with nuclear weapons and sporadically engaged in a shooting war over claims to the beautiful mountainous region of Kashmir. Our interviews with the leader of each nation, Prime Ministers Rajiv Ghandi in India and Muhammed Zia-al-Haq in Pakistan, focused on the tenuous relationship between the two countries and the potential for catastrophe should those relations break down. Both leaders were emphatic in declaring that their nuclear weapons were for deterrence only and would never be used offensively. Neither felt that the conflict over Kashmir posed any risk of expansion.

The careers of these two men evidence the perils of leadership in societies where succession is so often accompanied by bloodshed. Ghandi, the Cambridge-educated eldest son of Indira Ghandi, became India's sixth and, at age forty, youngest prime minister after the 1984 assassination of his mother. His tenure ended with his own assassination at the hands of Tamil separatists in 1991. Zia, an army general, deposed Ali Bhutto in a 1977 coup to become Pakistan prime minister and subsequently executed him. He was killed with several of his top generals and two U.S. diplomats a year after our interview in an apparently sabotage-caused plane crash.

At the time of our visit, Peshawar, the fabled Pakistan city below the Khyber Pass was crowded with refugees from the war Afghanistan tribesmen had been fighting for eight years against the Soviet army. They were easy to spot—men clumping around on one leg, children missing hands—maimed by land mines sown from Soviet planes. On a dusty Peshawar street, the Afghan Surgical Hospital housed the most severely injured. Some without eyes, some with faces burned away, some with brain or internal damage, they lay in crowded wards, stolidly waiting for healing through surgical or medical skills, time, and faith. Especially faith. Twice a day everything stopped as staff and all patients able to do so moved to the courtyard and knelt with foreheads to the ground, facing Mecca. Those who couldn't kneel turned in their beds.

These were warriors in what their Muslim leaders called a jihad, a holy war, men qualified to testify to the message of the Arabic banner hanging above the courtyard:

Desperation is only for unbelievers
Those who believe in God never lose heart

That thought echoed as I stood at the Khyber Pass, that ancient link between Central Asia and India. The invading army of Alexander the Great had crossed that pass. So had the Huns, then Tamerlane, then the Moguls. In more modern times, Britain fought and, like all the others, failed to subjugate the fiercely independent Afghan tribesmen. As I gazed from the pass into that troubled land and heard the distant roll of gunfire, memory recalled the poem of Rudyard Kipling about that effort:

When wounded you lie on Afghanistan's plains
And the women come out to cut up what remains,
Jest roll to your rifle and blow out your brains
An' go to your Gawd like a soldier.

Now it was the Russians' turn. Leonid Breznev ordered troops into Afghanistan in 1979 to support a Soviet-oriented government beleaguered by an uprising of the Pashton tribes, and to extend Soviet control deep into southern Asia and an eventual opening into the Arabian Sea. After nine years of fighting, 15,000 Russian and a million Afghan deaths, and with his own Soviet empire crumbling, the pragmatic Mikhail Gorbachev called it quits.

The last Soviet troops left Afghanistan in February 1989. Just over twelve years later, after the horrific September 11 attack on the World Trade Center, U.S. troops took their place. Our stated objective was to protect against future attacks by destroying Al

Qaeda, believed to be responsible for the attack and head-quartered in Afghanistan. Another objective was to replace the fundamentalist and perhaps terrorist-tolerant government there with one more favorable to the West.

The irony is unsettling. The Soviets invaded to prop up a government they could strongly influence if not control. Our purpose was the same. After nine years, baffled by the fierce independence of the Afghans, drained of manpower and treasure, with opposition mounting at home, the Russians left in defeat. After thirteen years of the same, we have essentially left as well. It remains for history to tell whether the final result will be different.

After Pakistan, the group of editors disbanded, and I returned to India. In Calcutta, I visited Mother Teresa's Home for the Dying. Stretcher cots crowded the floor, most occupied by men picked up off the streets and brought here to die in a semblance of dignity. Light filtering through the few dusty windows barely dispelled the gloom of this dingy place. Unforgettable was the smell of death. But more unforgettable was the sight of a beautiful girl holding in her arms and whispering love and encouragement to a dying man. A shaft of sunlight through a hole in the roof lit her blond hair like a halo. She was here on spring break from her school in Britain, she told me, but declined to give her name. "It's not about me," she said. "It's about these men, who deserve to die knowing they are loved and wanted." I left, pondering how sad is so much of the human condition, but how noble are those who care.

My last experience in India involved death as well, but in a vastly different way. I met a young man named Raj Kumar who had been attracted by the Young Ambassadors, a touring group of entertainers from Brigham Young University, had investigated the LDS Church, and become one of India's early converts.

Together, we drove 150 miles north of Delhi to the pilgrimage city of Haridwar. Considered by the Hindus to be one of their seven holiest cities, it straddles the Ganges River where it emerges from the Himalayas onto the Indo–Gangetic Plain. For centuries, millions of Hindus have come there for ritualistic bathing in the holy water of the Ganges, for open-fire cremation of their dead, and to cast into the river those ashes or the ashes they brought with them. On an early-morning run, with no one about, I took my own Ganges bath, acutely aware of the deep layer of bone fragments beneath my feet.

In this place exists a sect of Hindu Brahmin priests known as Pandits. Their role is and for centuries has been to record and preserve the names and ancestries of persons so honored. In a way I never understood, my friend Kumar was directed to the particular Pandit where his ancestry would be found. We met with him in his eight-foot-square cubicle, its walls covered floor to ceiling with pigeon holes holding hundreds of scrolls. Kumar gave the name of a grandfather and received a mild rebuke for not knowing more. The Pandit searched briefly, then unrolled scrolls containing the names and death dates of seven generations of ancestors. I was astonished. Kumar was more than that. Deeply moved, with tears in his eyes after copying the names, he declared, "I felt the spirit of Elijah."

The reason we were there was to do a story about the two-man Utah team of specialists in Haridwar to microfilm the thousands of scrolls stored there for adding to the LDS Church's vast genealogical library. I knew that the Church's store of such records was the world's largest, but not until this experience did I really appreciate the great effort it had taken to build it.

The final leg of this trip was not for the newspaper but to realize a long-held personal dream. Donna flew by way of Bangkok to meet me in Kathmandu, Nepal, for three weeks of trekking in the Himalayas. Up and down stone steps and over swinging foot bridges on trade trails built centuries ago, through miles of blooming rhododendron forests, up close with residents of the tiny villages clinging to the mountainsides, we trekked to camp at 18,000 feet at the Annapurna base camp, with another 8,500 feet of ice-clad mountain towering above us.

Of all the memories of that trek, two are special. One is the way our sherpas quietly appeared alongside at difficult or dangerous places on the trail, gave any needed help, then quietly slipped away expecting no thanks. That seems a model for the way we should give help when needed. The other memory is the greeting received from every person, young or old, encountered on the trail. With head bowed over folded hands came the greeting "Namaste"—meaning, we were told, "I greet the divine in you." How different might our Western society be if our greetings, and attitudes towards strangers, were like that?

An End and a New Beginning

On July 1, 1988, forty years to the day since I arrived at the Deseret News, I cleaned out my desk and walked away from an unintended career that had been sometimes frustrating, often fun, always challenging, almost always rewarding. I left it with no sense of bitterness and with gratitude for association with inspired and inspiring leaders and dedicated fellow workers, for the great diversity of people, places, and experiences I had encountered, and for the satisfaction that occasionally I had made a difference.

In India, and with Donna at Mount McKinley

CHAPTER TEN

Retirement? What's That?

R etirement enabled me to return to at least the fringes of a career I had intended to follow before being sidetracked into journalism—the researching and writing of history. The first effort produced *Old Utah Trails* (1988), the history of eight historic trails through or in Utah, from the Dominguez-Escalante Expedition (1776) to the Hole-in-the-Rock Expedition (1879-80). With a camp outfit and sleeping bag in the back of a Toyota 4-Runner purchased to replace my ancient green Blazer, I followed every one of those trails. Among other adventures, that involved a gimpy-legged author scrambling down the icy Hole-in-the-Rock three weeks after arthroscopic knee surgery in order to do it on January 26, 1987, 107 years to the day since the pioneers made their descent.

Chairmanship of the Friends of KUED led to the next book, *UTAH: A Portrait* (1995), conceived as a joint project of University of Utah Press and KUED. With the stunning photography of John Telford, it became a coffee table book, its text used in a subsequent KUED documentary. It includes the geological history of the land, guided by my friend, the esteemed University of Utah geology professor Lee Stokes; the human history from Archaic times to the present, and a loving description of the land itself, each section including a sidebar of a personal experience in that area. The success of this collaboration with Telford led to a similar but much less ambitious one, *Lake Powell: A Different Light* (1994), the history and present condition of Glen Canyon.

Donna caught the history virus and produced her own prizewinning book, *Mormon Midwife* (1997), based on the journals of the early pioneer midwife Patty Sessions. It won the

Evans Handcart Award for biography that year. She followed that with *Exemplary Elder* (2002), the biography of Patty's son Perrigrine, the founder of Bountiful.

Donna's passion for family history led to a book we produced together. Her great-great-grandfather William Henrie was a scout and hunter with Brigham Young's 1847 Pioneer Company. He then became part of Parley P. Pratt's fifty-man midwinter expedition of 1849-50, sent by Brigham to explore the length of what would be Utah to identify places for Mormons to settle. Henrie left no written account of what became a difficult and dangerous journey, but four others did. Searching for information about her ancestor, Donna read and transcribed all four of their handwritten journals. That led to our joint production of *Over the Rim: The Parley P. Pratt Exploring Expedition to Southern Utah, 1849-50*. It won the Mormon History Association award for Best Documentary Editing Award of 2000.

My own grandfather's career led to my most challenging book effort. His was a unique and fascinating life. Tortured in his early childhood by failures and guilt over inability to kick his tobacco addiction, he was called in his mid-thirties into church service that included presiding, in turn, over four LDS stakes, being the pioneer leader in Mormon settlement of the Uinta Basin, and wearing out his life as well as his fortune in the effort to make it Mormon Country. An inveterate journal-keeper, he left fifty volumes of journals that were passed down to me.

We recruited many of his descendants to help transcribe those journals, which were put on a single searchable CD. With the journals as a primary source, I wrote *Mormonism's Last Colonizer: The Life and Times of William H. Smart* (2008). The CD, containing 10,000 pages of journal, was inserted inside the back cover of the book. Allaying doubts expressed by some that an unbiased book could be written about one's own grandfather, it won both the Mormon History Association and the Evans Handcart 2008 awards for biography.

Post-Retirement Employment

Two part-time jobs, each radically different from the other, occupied the early years of my retirement. One was the editorship of *This People*, a Mormon-oriented magazine that up to that time had been chiefly known for its personality pieces on the rich and famous. I agreed to become its editor only on condition that we change it completely to a magazine of depth and purpose. In the editor's column of the first issue I wrote: "In reflecting the LDS lifestyle, we intend to do it realistically, honestly. Problems and shortcomings won't be ignored [but] the purpose will always be to be helpful, to seek solutions, to make a positive difference."

Our first issue (Spring 1988) set the tone. For some months I had been meeting with a small group pulled together by Ian Cumming, a wealthy non-Mormon entrepreneur concerned about the increasing polarization between Utah Mormons and their non-Mormon neighbors. We commissioned what proved to be an eye-opening survey of the attitudes of both groups and reasons for negative attitudes. This study and weeks of our group discussing possible solutions led to a groundbreaking *This People* magazine article: "LEAVING THEM OUT? Do Mormons Make Good Neighbors?" It made a difference. A July 7 letter from LDS headquarters that year cited problems of shunning and indifference the study revealed and appealed to stake presidents and bishops to "make friendshipping a matter of commitment by members within your area of responsibility." That emphasis continues to this day.

Another challenging article, written by our daughter Kristen Rogers, was "Stewards of the Earth" (Spring 1990), attempting through both ancient and modern scripture to raise Mormons' consciousness of our responsibility to care for this planet, our home. Much has been written about that since then, and progress has been made. But we still have a long way to go.

Four satisfying, though hardly profitable, years of editing *This People* ended when Donna and I were called in 1992 to serve an LDS Public Affairs mission covering eastern Canada, New England, and upstate New York. The magazine folded not long after.

The other, simultaneous part-time retirement job immersed me in unfamiliar waters. A friend and neighbor, Wayne Brown, dean of the College of Engineering at University of Utah, had become a sort of modern-day Johnny Appleseed, traveling around the country and often abroad, preaching and teaching the gospel of technological innovation and entrepreneurship. With that experience, he and a few associates established the Utah Innovation Foundation to carry on this work. They recruited me in 1985 to be its president.

My protests that I knew little about technology and less about entrepreneurship were brushed aside. They urged that my experience in resolving conflicts, building bridges, and thinking outside the box was what they needed. With confidence in Wayne Brown, admiration for what he was doing, and offer of a part-time salary that was little more than token, I came aboard.

Along with ongoing encouragement on and assistance to start-up companies, our major efforts were two. One was organizing and holding annually what we called the International Technological Innovation and Entrepreneurship Symposium. I conducted the first one in Salt Lake City in 1985 and others in Birmingham, England (1987), Brisbane, Australia (1988), and Minneapolis (1989). A highlight of the Brisbane symposium was the keynote address by 46-year-old Wan Hunnan, known as the most prominent and successful capitalist spawned by Deng Hsiao-ping's drive to modernize China in what he called the "Second Long March." Donna and I visited him and toured his Stone Computer Company plant in Beijing during our 1988 China visit, and were dismayed a year later when he was accused as a dissident behind the demonstrations that led to the Tienanmen Square massacre. He escaped the country to live in France and, later, Northern California.

The other major program of the foundation was the organizing and holding of an annual venture capital conference. We invited entrepreneurs with emerging companies that needed capital to submit their business plans. From these we selected the half-dozen or so of what seemed the most promising prospects. Mentor teams of venture experts worked with them to polish their business plans and rehearsed them on the presentations they would make to venture capitalists from around the country who attended the conference.

Sadly, Wayne Brown, the genius behind all this, was killed with his wife, son, daughter-in-law, and grandchild in 1988 when a deadly wind shear sent the plane he was attempting to land plunging to the ground. We renamed the foundation the Wayne Brown Institute, and carried on. Thinking big, I proposed we establish the Wayne Brown Chair of Technological Entrepreneurship at the University of Utah and make the holder director of the Institute, serving at the pleasure of its board. Chase Petersen, president of the University and a close friend, agreed with the concept, and I won the tentative agreement of

James Fletcher, former president of the university and director of NASA, to hold the position. Opposition to what was seen as loss of faculty control proved insurmountable, and the idea died.

The Wayne Brown Institute did not, however. Successful from the start, its venture capital conferences have grown steadily in outreach and results. The Institute's current website speaks of more than 300 companies assisted over the years and of 400 million dollars of venture capital invested in companies at the conference in the most recent four years.

My own venture capital career was somewhat less successful. Confident that among these exciting entrepreneurs there must be a Steve Jobs or two, I invested modestly in half a dozen companies that seemed most promising. Not one ever paid a dime of dividend, and none survives today. Shortly after the 1989 Minneapolis symposium, I realized that since I was no longer excited about this and the Institute could get along very well without me, I should resign. So I did.

A commitment from which I did not resign, but which increasingly occupied my retirement was to the responsibility we all share to be stewards of the earth, the subject of the following chapter.

CHAPTER ELEVEN

Stewardship of the Earth

On September 13, 1996, a Friday, the phone rang at Grand Canyon Trust headquarters in Flagstaff. The White House was on the line. Could the Trust organize and host a program at the South Rim of the Grand Canyon the following Wednesday as part of a special announcement (creation of the Grand Staircase – Escalante National Monument, it turned out) to be made by President Clinton and Vice President Gore?

The Trust could and did. Staff worked around the clock the next four days arranging the program, handling media inquiries and arrangements, printing and distributing 2,000 invitations, even preparing special Grand Canyon Trust T-shirts with "Clinton-Gore, Grand Canyon, Sept 18, 1996" on the back.

Trust president Geoff Barnard asked me, as a member of the board of directors, to introduce Vice President Gore, who would speak and then introduce the president. To my relief, two days later the White House superseded that decision; Norma Matheson, also a Trust director, would do the introduction in view of the close friendship she and her late husband Scott enjoyed with the Clintons while both were serving as governors. Instead, I was asked to speak briefly and introduce a dozen local environmental heroes who had done significant work on different conservation causes.

The big day, Sept 18, was a memorable and historic one. The crowd filled every inch of fenced-off space between El Tovar Hotel and the canyon's south rim. During a two-hour wait for arrival of the president's party, I visited with various government officials, especially Secretary of Interior Bruce Babbitt, with whom I had become well acquainted when he was a Trust board member before going to Washington. He asked me what

144

the president could do to make creation of the Grand Staircase – Escalante National Monument more palatable to Utahns. I told him that for many years Utah had been trying, futilely, to trade its school trust lands for more accessible and usable sections of federal lands. The best thing President Clinton could do, I said, would be to pledge to complete these trades, not only for lands included in the new monument but also for trust lands locked inside federal land throughout the state. Babbitt phoned Air Force One with this suggestion to the president's staff, who were still working on his message.

Our program went off well, including a Native American prayer by Vernon Masayesva, a Hopi member of the Trust board; my presentation in which, in addition to environmentalists nominated by the Trust staff, I recognized Mike Matz and Ken Rait of the Southern Utah Wilderness Alliance for their leadership of the Utah Wilderness Alliance's campaign for 5.7 million acres of BLM wilderness in Utah (the next day Matz whined to Barnard that SUWA had been ignored in the program); and brief talks by actor Robert Redford, writer-naturalist Terry Tempest Williams, and Trust board member Charles Wilkinson, a professor of law at the University of Colorado, the manuscript of whose book, *Fire on the [Colorado] Plateau*, I had read and critiqued.

Then, to much fanfare, the presidential party arrived. After Norma Matheson's introduction, Gore, who had authored the classic book *A World in the Balance*, spoke with as much passion as he ever shows about the administration's environmental record and then introduced "our environmental president."

Clinton spoke about visiting the Canyon in 1971, sitting for two hours on a rock looking into its depths and at the sunset. "Today, 25 years later," he said, "in hectic, crazy times, in lonely, painful times, my mind drifts back to those two hours that I was alone on that rock watching the sunset over this canyon; it will be with me till the day I die. I want more of those sights to be with all Americans for all time to come."

He then announced, by executive order, creation of the Grand Staircase – Escalante National Monument, 1.7 million acres of the Colorado Plateau between Kanab and the Colorado River and filling all the land (except around the towns of Tropic, Henrieville, Cannonville and Escalante) between Kanab and Highway 89 on the west, Bryce Canyon National park and Dixie National Forest on the north to Capitol Reef National Park and

Glen Canyon National Recreation Area on the east and south. No monument of such size had previously been created under the Antiquities Act of 1906, though what became Grand Canyon National Park was first protected by Theodore Roosevelt under that act in 1908. Bryce, Zion, Arches, and Capital Reef national parks in Utah were first protected that way. So were places like Grand Teton, Death Valley, and Olympic national parks.

To make the monument more acceptable to Utah's Congressional delegation and southern Utahns, Clinton put administration of the monument not under the National Park Service but under the Bureau of Land Management, with grazing, hunting, fishing, hiking, and camping continuing as before. The proclamation claimed no federal water rights. One thing it did do was prevent development of coal claims on the Kaiparowits Plateau by the Dutch-owned Andalex mining company—development that would have punched haul roads through proposed wilderness areas and sent huge trucks rumbling through southern Utah towns every five minutes to get coal to railheads in Moapa or Lund for shipment, primarily to Japan.

Clinton promised to expedite trades of Andalex leases for coal leases elsewhere. He also promised to trade Utah school lands in the monument for federal lands of equal or greater value and to expedite trades of other school lands throughout the state for more accessible federal land—a promise, Babbitt told me later, that was included at the last hour because of my suggestion. Some of those trades have since been made—notably the trade of federal lands around St. George for wilderness-quality school lands in the region—but not nearly enough. Some 3.5 million acres of school trust lands remain in Utah, more than a million of them in potential wilderness areas.

Even with these concessions, creation of the monument brought a firestorm of criticism from Utah's Congressional delegation, the media, and especially Southern Utah county and local officials, and it led to the defeat of Bill Orton, Utah's lone Democratic Congressman, in whose district the monument lies. Words like "outrageous land grab," "felonious assault," and "treacherous move against our children and this state" floated through Utah news stories and editorials, reminiscent of and about as farsighted as an editorial in the *Arizona Sun* that called Roosevelt's creation of Grand Canyon National Monument in 1908 "a fiendish and diabolical scheme....The fate of Arizona depends exclusively on the development of her mineral resources."

Creation of the monument, with the prestige the Grand Canyon Trust earned in organizing the event, was one highlight of the Trust's activities in the first eleven years of its existence, and certainly in the ten years since former Secretary of Interior Stewart Udall recruited me to be Utah's first representative on its board of trustees. Others on that initial board, besides Udall, included former Arizona Governor Bruce Babbitt, who would become Bill Clinton's Secretary of Interior. Scott Momaday, the noted Native American poet, would join the board in the next few years, as would Utahns Chase Petersen, Norma Matheson, Steven Snow, Lou Callister, and Owen Olpin and other outstanding people from throughout the country. Jim Trees, a New York financier and later a fruit rancher on the South Fork of the Virgin just south of Zion National Park, was a founder and the first chairman; Edward M. Norton, with whom I have especially enjoyed hiking Canyon Country, the first president.

How did I come to be involved with such people? Probably from a combination of two reasons. One is an ethic taught me since childhood: always leave a place better than you found it. (My wife Donna is an unyielding practitioner of that ethic; unforgettable is the sight of her picking toilet paper out of the sand and off bushes in a Lake Powell side canyon.)

Combine that ethic with love of the Colorado Plateau, especially its canyon country. As described earlier, that love was born the day in 1950 when we managed to wrestle a sedan up a jeep track into what would become Arches National Park. It blossomed under the tutelage of Bates Wilson, the superintendent of Arches National Monument. He started exploring the region surrounding the confluence of the Green and Colorado River in the early 1950s, became convinced it should be a national park, and took me camping and exploring there to discover why and join his campaign. Another camping trip with the noted painter Lynn Fausett and his wife taught us to see the splendor of that country through artist eyes. Never forgotten is the morning on that trip when I arose from my sleeping bag to the clear, descending notes of a canyon wren and gazed out over an ocean of Globe Mallow framed by the incredible spires of the Maze. In the years since then, Easter weekends and Utah Education Association breaks in October often found our family camping in the canyonlands.

By then, I was firmly committed to the preservation of such country. So when Stewart Udall in his recruiting visit explained that the mission of the Grand Canyon Trust was "to protect the canyon country of the Colorado Plateau—its spectacular landscapes, flowing rivers, clean air, diversity of plants and animals, and areas of beauty and solitude," I didn't hesitate.

Udall had long been one of my heroes. As President Kennedy's Secretary of Interior he had been instrumental in creating not only Canyonlands National Park but also the North Cascades and Redwoods national parks, the Appalachian National Trail, and four national monuments. He had been the moving force in creation of the Clean Air and Water, Wilderness, Endangered Species, Wild and Scenic Rivers, and Water Conservation acts. I felt deeply honored to join him on the Grand Canyon Trust board of directors. The fifteen years I served there were among the most rewarding times of my life.

A few weeks after the Monument creation, Utah governor Mike Leavitt asked to meet with the Trust board. With his aide, LaVarr Webb, he flew down to Pack Creek Ranch near Moab during an early blizzard and met with us for a couple of hours. He asked the Trust to take the lead in breaking the impasse and bitter controversy over designation of Utah BLM wilderness. He proposed an incremental approach, focusing first on non-controversial areas and then moving on to more difficult ones. I raised two objections: First, this approach would gradually reduce the passion and energy of the pro-wilderness movement as the more obvious pieces of wilderness were protected. Second, this would give Southern Utah county commissioners time and opportunity to continue their strategy of invalidating potential wilderness by bulldozing roads there. I told the governor the Trust could not consider supporting his approach unless he pledged to use the power of his office to prevent such desecration. He didn't, so the Trust and other environmental groups gave the proposal no support. The wilderness controversy continues with no end in sight.

The wilderness issue led to both satisfying and frustrating experiences that culminated in publication of an environmental book. In 1997 I was asked to represent the Grand Canyon Trust in testifying before the House and Senate public lands subcommittees. For the House hearing, held in the Utah State Capitol, the hearing room was packed, with many people standing. After members of Governor Leavitt's administration and some of the state's congressional delegation spoke against expansion of wilderness, five of us were invited to speak in favor of the bill then before Congress to protect 5.7 million acres of BLM wilderness. In my testimony I cited, among other arguments, a poll commissioned by the Trust that showed overwhelming support among Utahns for the additional wilderness. I ended with a statement by LDS President Gordon B. Hinckley that he had authorized me to use:

Here is declared the Creator of all that is good and beautiful. I have looked at majestic mountains rising against a blue sky and thought of Jesus, the creator of heaven and earth. I have stood on a spit of sand in the Pacific and watched the dawn rise like thunder—a ball of gold surrounded by clouds of pink and white and purple—and thought of Jesus, the Word by whom all things were made...What then shall you do with Jesus that is called Christ? This earth is his creation. When we make it ugly, we offend him.

"Please," I appealed to the committee members, "don't be a party to making it ugly." That brought a prolonged standing ovation from the predominantly pro-wilderness crowd.

The Senate hearing, a month later in the nation's capital, was somewhat less satisfying. Indeed, it was a fiasco. By the time a parade of anti-wilderness speakers were finished, the room was virtually empty. The media had gone, and the only senator left to hear testimony from Terry Tempest Williams and me was a lame duck from Oregon. Over dinner with Terry and her husband Brooke at our home a week later, we lamented the fact that the state administration and our entire congressional delegation were anti-wilderness, and that Utah and the LDS Church were seen as anti-environment. What could be done, we pondered, to identify and promote a Mormon environmental ethic? That night, the book Terry and I did together with Gibbs Smith, *New Genesis: A Mormon Reader on Land and Community*, was conceived.

We recruited forty Mormons of widely different backgrounds and points of view, each to write an essay on our relationship to and stewardship for the land. Each essay was prefaced by a relevant scripture, some from the Bible, more from the Book of Mormon, Doctrine and Covenants, and Pearl of Great Price. Quotations from Joseph Smith, Brigham Young, Spencer W. Kimball, and Gordon B. Hinckley demonstrated what once was and could again be a Mormon environmental ethic. My own essay, "The Making of an Activist," described the mentors, the experiences, and the beauty and power of the land itself that changed a Mormon Republican working for a conservative newspaper into a dedicated environmentalist. Reviewer Jerry Johnson of the *Deseret News* called *New Genesis* a "landmark" and the book of the year. We hoped it would change the stance of Church leaders and members toward earth stewardship, and public perception of that stance, but saw little evidence that it did.

In other ways I made a difference, though. In 1990, my second year on the Grand Canyon Trust board, while flying home from a board meeting in Flagstaff, I had what I feel was an epiphany. Until that time, the Trust had been entirely issue-oriented, fighting for protection of the Colorado Plateau through lobbying efforts in Washington and, when necessary, litigation. Results had been limited, though we were making progress in what resulted in a forced agreement to clean up the air pollution from the giant coal-fired power plant at Page, Arizona.

My flash of insight was that we could accomplish far more by collaborating with communities and resource users on the Plateau, educating and building consensus for responsible development and environmental protection, using litigation only as a last resort. I outlined my thoughts in a letter to the leadership.

It took more than a year for the concept to percolate through the organization, but it was finally adopted. To launch it, I recruited the cooperation of Gerald Sherratt, president of Southern Utah University, and helped organize what became the "Colorado Plateau Community Initiatives Symposium: Coping with Change, Economy and the Environment." For three days at the university, September 18-20, more than 150 government and community leaders and resource users met with academicians and environmental activists trying to figure out how to sustain ourselves economically without trashing the place we love. The 143-page publication of the proceedings contains this acknowledgment: "The Community Initiatives Program has developed from ideas expressed by Bill Smart, a member of the Board of Trustees. His initial vision that community leaders could be brought together to work productively to incorporate responsible conservation into local decision-making has guided this effort from the beginning."

On that foundation, the Trust has built an increasingly successful record of resource protection. Some board members were initially skeptical. That approach, they felt, would dry up funding; only an issue-based adversarial approach would attract big donors. That was far from true; annual revenue grew from around $300,000 at the time of the Symposium to more than $3,000,000 by the time I left the board.

Though my work on the Trust board was in the area of policy and program development rather than fundraising, I got involved there as well. One of the Trust's tactics was to take potential big contributors on Colorado River float trips through the Grand Canyon with a few Trust board and staff members. After participating in one of them, I suggested they could get a more intimate and compelling understanding of the scale, diversity, and protection challenges of this magnificent country by backpacking through it.

Led by my nephew and his wife, BYU former survival program guides Tom and Kim DeLong, my wife and I had twice hiked a four- or five-day point-to-point route down Coyote Gulch to the Escalante River, up the river to Stevens Canyon and its spectacular arch, then up that canyon to a point where we could climb out on frightening Moki steps to cross the Waterpocket Fold to a boat pickup where Halls Creek joins Lake Powell. It has all the elements of a great hike—exposure, some rope work, some swimming through deep slot canyons, waterpockets for an evening soak, canyon wrens to serenade the sunrise, and, of course, magnificent scenery. It would make, I urged, an ideal introduction of potential contributors to the heart of the Colorado Plateau. So, of course, I was asked to lead such a hike.

We had some great people: Ed Norton, president of the Trust; and five big-hitter prospects, including Pulitzer Prize-winning writer/historian David Halberstam. Also included was Hansjorg Wyss, a Swiss entrepreneur who had built a fortune developing and marketing medical appliances. At hike's end he wrote a large check to the Trust—$50,000 as I recall—and shortly after became a board member and treasurer. In subsequent years, through his large annual grants from the permanent foundation he established to support its work, he has been by far the Trust's largest individual contributor.

With its philosophy of positive collaboration rather than negative confrontation, the Trust has accomplished much. In 2000, it was instrumental in persuading former Trust board member and now Secretary of Interior Bruce Babbitt, and ultimately President Clinton, to double the size of the Grand Canyon

– Parashant National Monument to 1,054,000 acres, including the entire Arizona Strip watershed draining into this section of the Colorado. With the earlier Grand Staircase – Escalante National Monument and a few smaller ones, over three million acres of the Colorado Plateau have been given this special protection. By purchasing grazing rights from willing sellers, the Trust has removed cattle from 385,000 acres and 150 miles of streams, allowing them to recover after more than a century of abuse. Its continuing campaign to clean up the air pollution spewing from coal-fired power plants has resulted in emission controls on three of the plants and shut down completely the biggest polluter, the Mohave plant in Laughlin, Nevada. Years of persistence finally persuaded Congress to fund the removal of sixteen million tons of uranium waste threatening to wash into and poison the Colorado River near Moab. There has been much more, including forest restoration and work with Indian tribes on community-based development and renewable energy projects.

But by far the Trust's biggest project was the 2005 purchase of the Kane and Two-Mile ranches on the Arizona Strip after negotiations that started while I was a board member. The Nature Conservancy joined in the purchase, but the Trust manages the project. It is a huge one. The ranches with their grazing allotments cover 850,000 acres, spreading from a 110-mile common border with Grand Canyon National Park on the south to Paria Creek on the north and from Kanab Creek on the west across House Rock Valley to Lees Ferry on the east. From a 3,000-foot elevation in the bottom of Paria Canyon it rises through various ecological life zones to the ponderosa and spruce forests at a 9,000-foot elevation on the Kaibab. Much of the land has been badly overgrazed. Through reduced livestock numbers and scientific study and management, the Trust aims not only to restore the land and its wildlife but also to establish guidelines and methods that will encourage sustainable ranching elsewhere. Each summer, 250 or so volunteers participate in the study and restoration projects.

In 1998, the Grand Canyon Trust board adopted a limit of three three-year terms, so, having already served four terms, I left the board. Three years later, I accepted an invitation to rejoin. But after one more term, at age 82 and with the contacts and influence I had developed during my newspaper career mostly gone, I felt a younger person could be more effective. My resignation ended fifteen years of challenging, happy and, I feel, difference-making service.

My work with the Trust led to other satisfying conservation activities. In 1994 I was asked to become a director of the Southwest Heritage Foundation, interested in archaeological exploration and land conservation in the Bluff area. In that capacity I obtained from the George and Dolores Eccles Foundation a challenge grant to purchase and save from subdivision development eight acres of land between the historic Bluff cemetery and the excavation site of an outlying Anazasi great house of the Chaco Canyon culture.

From the same foundation, through long friendship with Spencer Eccles, David Gardner and other foundation directors, I helped obtain grants for two other projects on behalf of the Trust. One was a one-for-two challenge grant to preserve the Mormon pioneer ghost town of Grafton on the Virgin River. The project not only protected the townsite and stabilized its buildings but also purchased 210 acres surrounding the site. This saved the area from subdivision and commercialization on the approach to Zion National Park and turned it into a nature preserve instead. Project cost: $1.3 million. The other was to purchase acreage at the confluence of Calf Creek with the Escalante, preserving that beautiful area from future commercial development.

Work on the Trust also led to my appointment by Secretary of Interior Babbitt as a charter member of the Utah BLM Resource Advisory Council, representing the environmental community. I served two three-year terms and was gratified that, through study and respectful but often vigorous debate between the competing interests represented on the RAC, we succeeded in hammering out balanced and acceptable Standards and Guidelines for grazing on BLM lands, for rehabilitation of lands burned in rangeland fires, and finally for recreational use of the public lands, including that of off-highway vehicles. Sadly, much of what we achieved was lost in the environment-destructive policies of the George W. Bush administration.

My concern about earth stewardship didn't end, though. In 2006 Jerrold N. Willmore, a returned missionary but no longer active LDS, wrote an op-ed piece for the *Tribune* calling on the LDS Church to join other churches in urging action to avert the impending crisis of global warming and climate change. I called to congratulate him and found a passionate, energetic, and well-informed activist on the issue. I agreed to meet with him to discuss what might be done. Two others joined us—Scott Daniels, a former legislator and chair of the Utah State Bar, and Sidney J. Nebeker, founder of a high-tech company serving an international market. I suggested that a general conference address on the subject by one of the general authorities might help, but not much; what was really needed was a proclamation like the Church's powerful, widely distributed 1995 Proclamation on the Family—this one a Proclamation on the Health of the Earth. That became our goal.

We met weekly for several months, debating strategy and assembling materials for the most impressive presentation we could manage. Fortuitously, in our condominium lived the most effective man we could have found to help. He was Robert S. Wood, a general authority Seventy. Before his full-time Church calling, he had been, among other positions, dean of the U.S. Navy War College Strategy Department and director of the Center for Naval Warfare Studies. Because of his understanding of world affairs and personal acquaintance with many of those involved, the Church did not grant him the normal emeritus retirement at age seventy. Instead, he was serving an additional five years as special adviser on the Public Affairs Committee and also the Area Committee. This little-known committee, composed of the Quorum of the Twelve, the seven presidents of the Seventy, and the Presiding Bishopric, reports directly to the First Presidency on matters beyond the usual ecclesiastical and organizational province of the Church. I outlined to him our purpose. He expressed support and outlined the strategy we should—and did—follow.

On June 29, 2006, we delivered to Russell M. Nelson, chairman, and to each member of the Public Affairs Committee a letter and a fat package of supporting material, including Al Gore's just-published book, *An Inconvenient Truth*, and Lester R. Brown's book, *Plan B: Rescuing a Planet Under Stress*, recommending they read chapter four of the latter, describing the depth and disastrous consequences of climate change, and chapter ten, outlining the many ways the problem could be and in some cases was being met. The letter I composed and ran by Elder Wood for approval was signed by us and three others I recruited to add weight to our request—former U. S. senator Jake Garn, University of Utah president Michael Young, and former U of U president Chase N. Petersen. The letter concluded with these words:

> We recognize and honor our Church's policy of speaking out only on important and carefully considered moral issues. It has done so—appropriately, we feel—on other environment-related issues, such as MX missile siting and storage of nuclear wastes. We regard global warming/climate change as a far more crucially important moral issue. The same Lord who created this bountiful, beautiful earth and pronounced it good has in our era, declared, "For it is expedient that I, the Lord, should make every man accountable, as a steward over earthly blessings, which I have made and prepared for my creatures. (DC 104:14).
>
> Now, it seems to us, is the time wise and pro-active stewardship is critically needed. Who can call for it more authoritatively than he who holds the keys of prophecy today? We hope—and pray—that our beloved First Presidency might be inspired to take this matter before the Lord, and that out of that inquiry might come a Proclamation on the Health of the Earth, calling on individuals, families, industry, and local, state, national, and international leadership to join in a comprehensive effort to curtail carbon dioxide emissions in defense of our earthly home.
>
> Sincerely your brethren

Elder Wood reported that the committee was scheduled to meet one hour, with ten items on the agenda, but instead spent an hour and a quarter discussing our request. A proposal was made that the committee should draft a statement for First Presidency approval. The more cautious decision was that Elder Nelson would discuss with the First Presidency whether it should go forward; if so, the committee would then prepare the statement.

Whether he did or not I do not know. For ten months we heard nothing. Then on May 3, 2007, came a "Dear Bill" letter from Elder Nelson. He thanked us for our letter and supporting materials, which, he wrote, "have been carefully reviewed. For the Church to become officially involved with a major social issue such as this is rare. Generally such involvement, if any, follows a very deliberate and time-consuming process." He then quoted a 1968 statement by the First Presidency: "The growing world-wide responsibilities of the Church make it inadvisable for the Church to seek to respond to all the various and complex issues involved in the mounting problems of the many cities and communities in which members live. But this complexity does not absolve members as individuals from filling their responsibilities in their own communities."

That sounded like a gentle way of telling us our appeal would not succeed—not surprising since major policy decisions in the Church's presiding councils require unanimity, while some people, especially among conservative Republicans, deny that burning of fossil fuels contributes to global warming. So we understood and accepted, but were puzzled that the inadvisability of responding to the "problems of many cities and communities in which members live" was cited as a reason not to respond to a threat to the entire planet.

Not quite ready to give up, I continued to nudge Elder Wood about having the matter brought before the Area Committee. After several more months, a meeting was scheduled to do so, on October 24, 2007. U of U president Michael Young, who had won the respect and confidence of Church leadership, and who had signed our original letter sixteen months earlier, was asked to make the presentation. Willmore, Daniels, and I met with him to share our views—and our passion—about what he might present. We found him already thoroughly prepared and competent.

Elder Wood had an out-of-state assignment and missed the meeting. But he reported the presentation was very effective, with much discussion. Subsequently, he informed me that Quorum of the Twelve president Boyd Packer "is thinking a lot about this issue, which means that the quorum members are thinking about it too." A few weeks later, he reported that, "You hit a home run; President Packer has talked to me five times about it." Since then, not a word. Elder Wood left to become president of the Boston Temple, and climate change doesn't seem to appear on Church headquarter radar screens.

Our efforts weren't entirely futile, however. Early in our campaign, Willmore and I, together with Salt Lake County Mayor Peter Corroon, met with Governor Jon Huntsman. We had two requests. The first was that he join us in signing the letter urging a Church proclamation on global warming. Though he applauded our effort, because of understandable and valid political concerns he declined.

The second request was that he organize a blue ribbon council to study the threat of global warming and recommend steps the state should take to meet it. Our meeting was in early June, 2006. On August 25 he announced the names of 24 industry, government, community, and environmental leaders appointed to a Blue Ribbon Advisory Council on Climate Change to do exactly that. In October 2007 the council issued its final report: Global warming is real, it declared, and burning of fossil fuels is almost certainly a cause. Embracing existing technologies and proven policies could increase Utah's energy efficiency 20% by 2015. It would save the state's residents, businesses, industries, and government agencies $7.1 billion in energy costs over that period, would reduce greenhouse gas emissions by 7.9 million tons, and save 3.4 billion gallons of water. The report listed 23 specific policies and technologies needed to accomplish that.

We have made modest progress on some of those. But Governor Huntsman left office to become ambassador to China, the voices of global warming deniers grow louder, and Huntsman's successor, Gary R. Herbert, if not a denier is a self-described skeptic. Hot times are ahead.

Hiking at the Wave, c. 2010

CHAPTER TWELVE

An Odyssey of Faith

In a church like mine, the Church of Jesus Christ of Latter-day Saints (Mormon), operated mainly by its lay members, the extent and nature of their service and the depth of their commitment to it become an essential part of who and what each of those members is. What does that say about me?

My church service began as a twelve-year-old deacon passing the sacrament in the Manavu Ward in Provo, followed by sweeping out the beer bottles and emptying the ash trays before preparing the sacrament in Dania Hall, where our tiny Reno congregation met. In the years since, I have been a seminary teacher, guide on Temple Square, teacher in various priesthood and Sunday School classes, chairman in turn of the M Men and Explorer committees of the Church-wide Young Men's Mutual Improvement Association general board (1949-1964); bishop of Federal Heights Ward (1964-69), high councilman, member of the Sunday School general board and its executive committee (1971-76), high priest group leader in Emigration and Ensign stakes, missionary with Donna directing Church public affairs in Eastern Canada, New England, and upstate New York (1992-94), and, again with Donna, ordinance worker in the Salt Lake Temple (until 2015).

I don't propose to describe this service in chronological or any other order, but to relate a few examples of how its experiences have taught and developed the principles and convictions that have shaped my life.

A core conviction is that among our greatest gifts, if not the greatest next to the atoning sacrifice of the Savior, is the gift of the Holy Ghost. Not only is it a sure guide to what is right and wrong, a testifier of God's reality and His love, and the divine establishment of His church, but also a comfort in time of trial, a source of strength and assurance when needed, and a prompter of things we ought or ought not to do. It helps, of course, to recognize those promptings and act on them. I have often failed to do so, but am learning.

In an earlier chapter I described the prompting that led to my greatest blessing, marriage to the beautiful, intelligent, highly principled and devout woman who changed my life. Looking back to that defining moment, I realize that this was the first time that I can remember experiencing the power of and being blessed by the whispering of the Holy Ghost.

There have been many others. Among the most important was the night out in the Pacific at the end of World War II. For the first time, I had begun to read, ponder, and pray about the Book of Mormon. As I lay in my bunk doing that, suddenly my whole body was suffused with warmth, and I knew the truth of what I was reading. That conviction has never left me. It grew when I returned to college and was asked to teach an investigators class. For the first time I felt the sweetness of service in the Church. For the first time I found it necessary to really study the scriptures and to pray for inspiration, and as a result felt increasingly the enlightenment and companionship of the Holy Ghost.

Some would say that the promptings we experience and their consequences can be explained as mere coincidence. I believe otherwise. One for which there is no possible explanation other than prompting from a heavenly source occurred in 1950. In those days, youth leaders from throughout the Church gathered in the annual three-day June conference of the Mutual Improvement Association. In the opening session of the 1950 conference, as a recently called general board member I sat with the board in the raised seats flanking the podium, in full view of the congregation that filled the Tabernacle. In the middle of someone's talk, I stood up and left.

I had no idea why I had done such a rude and unprecedented thing. I only knew I had to call home. I did and Donna answered, badly shaken after being broad-sided by a cement truck, worried about the safety of the baby in her womb, and facing the daunting challenge of being mistress of ceremonies and introducing President George Albert Smith as the speaker at the annual Golden Gleaner banquet that evening. After words of comfort and assurance and a priesthood blessing, she conducted the event beautifully, and six weeks later our first daughter, Melinda, was born healthy and beautiful. I have had many promptings of the Spirit before and since—and followed some of them—but none more unmistakable of the unseen power that blesses our lives.

It shouldn't be surprising that the most memorable promptings have been those enabling us to bless others. One Sunday afternoon, as bishop I sat in my office pondering how I could better serve our ward members. The prompting came clear: Call a certain young couple we had never seen inside the church and ask if they would come over for a talk. They came. I told them I was impressed that it was time for them to become active in the church. Through her tears the wife asked, "How could you have known we were praying about how we could?" As we discussed what was necessary and got to tithing, they hesitated. They were struggling financially, they said; that would be a problem. Yes, I replied; for those who don't pay tithing, it's one of the hardest commandments to keep. But I'll make you a promise. When you are paying it faithfully, you'll find it's the easiest.

A year later, suffering in her hospital bed from cancer, this good woman took my hand as I prepared to give the priesthood blessing she requested. "Bishop," she said, "remember the promise you made about tithing? It has been so true." That was in 1963. Fifty years later, cancer finally claimed her after a life so full of service it was acknowledged by the First Presidency in a letter of condolence read to her faithful family at her funeral.

As they often do, a prompting in 1993 led to unforeseen and, in this case, far-reaching results. As public affairs missionaries headquartered in Toronto, we were responsible for training and assisting stake public affairs councils in eastern Canada, New England, and upstate New York, and, of course, performing public affairs duties ourselves. One public affairs goal was—and is—to build interfaith relations. We did that in a small way by making friends with the pastor and some of his flock in a neighboring Presbyterian congregation and holding joint activities with a Jewish synagogue, but how to do it on a large scale we had no clue.

One day, Donna clipped from the *Globe and Mail* a small notice of a series of seminars on world religions. We decided to attend the next one. On the scheduled day, the heaviest snowstorm we experienced in two winters there hit Toronto, a city not unfamiliar with heavy storms. That night the streets were piled high with snow, and it was bitterly cold. The urge was strong to stay warm by the fire. But the prompting to go was stronger, so we went.

The topic that night was Hinduism. During a coffee break we introduced ourselves to the discussion leader, Paul Newman. His response was unforgettable: "Did you know you were prayed here? We are publishing a book on the churches of Canada, and we had no idea who we could get to write about the Mormons."

The book, *Faith in My Neighbor: World Religions in Canada*, published the following year, contains my chapter titled simply "Mormonism," sandwiched between "Judaism" and "Sikhism," but that's not the most important result of our prompting. Reverend Newman turned out to be the director of public outreach for the United Church of Canada. He became our friend and invaluable adviser. 1994 was the International Year of the Family, and we were in the early stage of planning a Mormon open house and family values exhibit at one of our chapels. Instead, at Newman's suggestion and with his involvement, we were able to play a leading role in organizing what grew into a three-day Interfaith Family Festival in the Toronto Metropolitan Museum of Art. Thirty-four other faiths joined ours with booths and exhibits. Months of planning meetings with representatives of those faiths did much to broaden our appreciation of their faiths and theirs of ours.

Another conviction that has grown throughout my life is that God hears and answers prayers. One among many examples came early in my time as chief editorial writer for the *Deseret News*. It was near the end of the day, and I was in trouble. As chairman of the Explorer committee I was due at a YMMIA board meeting in little more than an hour. Not only had I not written the next day's lead editorial, but I hadn't even been able to think of a subject. Becoming desperate, I bowed over my typewriter and prayed for help. A subject came immediately to mind, and I started typing. I have never before nor since written a lead editorial that fast, and certainly never one with less research. The result was an editorial entitled "No Smokescreens in Our Schools." It won a modest cash award and a plaque proclaiming it the nation's best editorial about education in 1953, but I have never considered myself more than its co-author.

Two things I have learned about prayer are that usually the requested assistance is provided through people, and that sometimes the result is far greater than requested or hoped for. A significant example of both came during our service as Public

Affairs missionaries in Canada.

A major part of our calling was to work with the media to convey to the public accurate and helpful information about the Church, and to bring the Church out of obscurity. We built good relations with the religion editors of Toronto's two major newspapers, the *Globe and Mail* and the *Star*, and in several instances were able to help them with their coverage. But about the other media, television, we knew little and had less influence. We prayed a lot about that.

The prayers were answered. One day, a church member called for an appointment to seek my counsel about launching a Mormon-oriented magazine. He asked if he could bring a friend. He did, and she turned out to be Joan Patrick, a convert of two months who had recently been given early retirement as senior editor in Canada's national television network. We immediately recruited her to join our regional Public Affairs Council, which probably set a new record for the shortest time after baptism to receive such a church calling. Our good friend, Apostle Neal A. Maxwell, happened to be in Toronto on Church business at the time, and we invited him to set Joan apart for this new calling. In doing so, he blessed her to have great influence in bringing the Church out of obscurity through Canadian television.

She certainly did. Through her expertise and contacts, we produced a series of half-hour telecasts, adapting existing Church videos to meet Canadian requirements. These aired monthly in prime time on the national faith network, which meant that the name of the Church and title of the program appeared monthly in newspaper TV guides throughout Canada. Our Easter offering, "The Lamb of God," scored the highest Nielsen rating ever at the time for a religion program on Canadian television. The series was repeated for several years after we returned home.

Even that wasn't the end of influence on Canadian TV resulting from the prayers that brought Joan Patrick to our door. Through contacts developed during the preparation and airing of those telecasts I was invited to join the board of the national faith network. Because our mission would soon end, I had to decline but suggested that Bruce Smith, by far the most effective regional representative with whom we worked in promoting public affairs, be invited instead. He was, accepted, and eventually served several years as the board's chairman.

In addition to the umbrella principles of faith, repentance, and obedience, other principles have shaped my life, at least those parts of my life that are good and worthy of the blessings I have received. One is the principle of eternal progression, a recognition of our limitless potential. I am especially moved by and grateful for those verses in Doctrine and Covenants 130 that promise us that whatever principles of intelligence we gain in this life will rise with us in the resurrection and will give us so much advantage in the world to come. Those verses tell me we had better stretch ourselves in this life. We'd better accept tough challenges and do our best. We'd better be proactive and create opportunities where none seem to exist. There's no better way to develop strength, knowledge, and faith. Moreover, such efforts have eternal consequences.

A companion principle, not scripture but profound, I discovered many years ago while prowling through Henry Ford's mansion in Fair Lane, by then converted into a museum. In a desk drawer were words scribbled on the back of an envelope. Could they have been written, I wondered, by the great industrialist himself? They were:

Dare to do more than you can do, and do it.
Bite off more than you can chew, and chew it.
Hitch your wagon to a star,
Keep your seat,
And there you are.

Finally, there's the truth I've discovered in Nephi's declaration when he was sent on a dangerous and seemingly impossible mission, that "the Lord giveth no commandments unto the children of men, save he shall prepare a way for them that they may accomplish the thing which he commandeth them." (1 Ne 3:7).

Assurances like these can lead to overly optimistic and unrealistic efforts and expectations, some of which are chronicled in these pages. But they have led to other projects, also chronicled here, with more satisfying results.

An especially satisfying one began when Bishop James Beck of our Federal Heights ward called Donna and me in 1997 to organize the ward's activities to celebrate the 150th anniversary of the arrival of Brigham Young's Pioneer Company in Salt Lake Valley. Church president Gordon B. Hinckley had requested every ward and stake to undertake a service project that year to improve its community. That's not exactly a commandment, but for a committed Mormon a request from the man we regard as a prophet it comes close.

As a trail historian and member of the stake sesqui-centennial coordinating council, I was aware that the site where the first Mormons camped in the valley, on July 22, had never been marked and was little-known. We proposed that our service project be to place a small monument there. Nearby, on the southwest corner of Seventeenth South and Fifth East, was a weed- and trash-filled vacant lot, formerly occupied by an Amoco service station. The vision expanded. Who more appropriately than our own Emigration Stake could build an historical heritage park there? Because the site was in the Wells Stake, we invited its members to join ours in voluntary labor. I took Salt Lake City mayor Deedee Corradini to the site, explained our plan, and said we were prepared to proceed if the city would own and manage the park and replace the deteriorated curb, gutter, and sidewalk at city expense. She agreed.

After weeks of delay because of concern over its size and cost, the stake president called a special stake priesthood meeting May 11 to consider the project. A high council member experienced in designing and monitoring church heritage sites told the body he fully supported it, but he warned that unless all plans were complete, with funding in place and a willingness to pay contractors a premium to fast-track the construction, there was no way it could be done by July 19, designated by President Hinckley as World Heritage Day. I replied that he was no doubt correct, but that in the spirit of the sesquicentennial theme of "Faith in Every Footstep," we intended to build it with volunteer labor and have it completed by that date within a modest budget of $75,000. It was, by any rational measure, an outrageous statement, but made in faith that if one commits to a worthy project, unselfishly and for the good of others, not caring who gets the credit, heaven will join in the effort. Miracles happen.

They did. One was that the funding was over-subscribed, 80 percent of it by members of our own Federal Heights Ward. Another was that Amoco donated the property. A third was the priceless work of stake member Stuart Loosli, a landscape architect. He donated hundreds of hours in designing the park, then supervising construction and shoveling more than his share of dirt.

From the several concepts he presented, we chose one that

involved piling 150 tons of granite boulders along the east edge of the park to represent the Wasatch Mountains. From them emerge dry stream beds representing Parleys and Emigration creeks, near the confluence of which the pioneers first camped. The names of the 120 persons who camped there that night are inscribed on granite boulders throughout the park. Walkways are of 6,800 multi-hued concrete paving bricks, every one painstakingly placed there by a volunteer on his or her knees. Generous suppliers donated or deeply discounted cement work, paving bricks, decorative light poles, fencing, sprinkling and electrical systems, and plant material.

But to me the most moving miracle was the commitment and enthusiasm that went into the 4,500 man- (and woman-) hours of volunteer labor needed to build the park. Climax of the work came, as requested by President Hinckley, on World Heritage Day, July 19. On that day, more than 200 volunteers accomplished miracles, installing the sprinkler system, laying 4,600 feet of sod, completing more than 500 plantings, installing four permanent benches, and cleaning up the entire site for the dedication to follow in three days.

On July 22, 1847, the main body of the Pioneer Company emerged from Emigration Canyon about 4 p.m. and followed Emigration Creek to the campsite. On that same date and hour in 1997, 450 members of the two stakes left from the same place and followed, as closely as possible, the same route. At 7 p.m., 150 years to the hour since the pioneers were lighting their cooking fires, began the program culminating in dedication of the park by Russell M. Ballard of the Twelve, chairman of the Church-wide sesquicentennial activities. The memorial hike has been held every year since.

Today, in our early nineties, Donna and I no longer conceive of, much less attempt, ambitious projects. We are happily content with the quiet life, grateful that, until the last couple of years, my considerately younger tennis buddies still tolerated my aging efforts, and that both of us still attempted what we laughingly call golf. After seventy-one years of marriage, we are grateful for each other and for the love and support of three generations of harmonious and capable family members. Looking back over all those years, we find comfort in the thought that occasionally we may have made a difference.

Portraying Joseph Smith for the MIA
general conference in 1962

Donna and Bill, 2013

Index

Utah-Bolivian Partnership. See National Association of the Partners of the Alliance
Utah Constitutional Revision Commission, 81
Utah Heritage Foundation, 64
Utah Humanities Council, 65, 82
Utah Innovation Foundation. See Wayne Brown Institute
Utah State Prison: riot in 1951, 43
Utah State University, 58, 61, 131; President Darryl Chase, 59
Utah Symphony Board, 81
Utah's United Nations Day Observance, 65
Valentine, Dan, 106
Van Atta, Dale, 84-85, 101, 104
Vanport flood, 31
Wan Hunnan, 142
Washington County News, 95
Wayne Brown Institute, 141-143
Webb, LaVarr, 104, 128, 148
Western States Arts Foundation, 82
Westminster College, 74-76
Williams, Terry Tempest, 145, 149
Willmore, Jerrold N., 153, 156
Wilkinson, Ernest L., 61-62
World War II, 20, 22-25, 31, 43, 47, 56, 59. See also Smart, William B.: military service
Wood, Robert S., 154-156
Woodford, Frank B., 50
Wyoming, 22-24, 27, 30
"You're the Editor," 91-92
Zia-al-Haq, Muhammed, 134